PAULINE DRUIFF is a divorced and remarried Christian. Following the breakdown of her marriage to an Anglican priest, she returned to work and was, for ten years, a PA with the General Synod. A founder member and past chairman of Broken Rites, a self-help group for separated and divorced wives of clergy, she co-compiled and edited *Broken Rites – The First Twenty Years*, produced by the group last year, and has had articles and poems published in parish magazines and insets nationally. She is a trained spiritual director. Pauline lives in Sussex with her second husband.

For
Ian and Ann

When Marriage Breaks Up

A Guide for Christians

Pauline Druiff

First published in Great Britain in 2004 by
Society for Promoting Christian Knowledge
Holy Trinity Church
Marylebone Road
London NW1 4DU

British Library Cataloguing-in-Publication Data

A catalogue record for this book is available from the British Library

ISBN 0-281-05676-5

1 3 5 7 9 10 8 6 4 2

Typeset by Avocet Typeset, Chilton, Aylesbury, Bucks
Printed in Great Britain by Bookmarque Ltd, Croydon, Surrey

Contents

Foreword

I first met the author of this personal, practical and deeply felt analysis of divorce, its causes and consequences, when her first husband, formerly in the Army and in business, came to Lincoln Theological College to be trained as an Anglican priest. Lincoln had a tradition of accepting married men for training but its ethos and spirituality were still monastic, and its discipline over hours of worship unimaginative for those who with their wives had the responsibility of a home and family.

During my time as Warden the college continued to buy as many houses near the college as it could, and gradually wives and children were welcomed to more services, meals and events. This contrasted with other more old-fashioned colleges, where wives were not allowed to live within two miles of their husband's room in college – the rule nicknamed 'The Principal's Safety Belt'. Gradually a more balanced community developed as the families got to know each other. Children were welcomed in the college grounds, which became more open. It was an accepting and generally happy community of about 100 men, women and children, and many of us made life-long friendships. But looking back it's clear that Lincoln ought to have made many radical changes more quickly.

The Church's teaching on sexual morality in the second half of the twentieth century was still in denial, even though society was changing rapidly. On homosexuality two farsighted reports, by Gresford Jones in 1953 and Osborne in 1989, were unfortunately never published. The main question on divorce was whether you could or could not be remarried in church and repeated debates took place in Synod. An Anglican layman, John Wolfenden, brought forward a government report to decriminalize gay relationships in civil society and Parliament accepted this, but there was little discussion in the churches of a new morality for gay and lesbian relations. Many assumed that authority at home and in the Church must be male, and much religious language was male. The decisions to ordain women in 1992 in the UK and to consecrate a gay bishop in the USA in 2003 are symbols of a new appreciation of a more tolerant sexuality.

In 1995 the Board for Social Responsibility produced a report: *Something to Celebrate: Valuing Families in Church and Society*. In the initial cultural survey entitled 'The Street Where You Live' the immense variety of family life in Britain today was illustrated. It quotes a woman in Sheffield: 'I long for a church that is not frightened of diversity and which recognizes several kinds of families.' Some church leaders scuttled for cover and reacted negatively, as if they wished the churches to go on saying 'Stop it' over and over and rather loudly. The Archbishop of Canterbury saw the authors of the report and behaved, one of them said, 'like a cross headmaster'. Today, in contrast to these reactions, the appended list of caring organizations includes Broken Rites, founded as a result of the interest of two Members of Parliament in helping divorced clergy wives, which reveals that the main response of the churches is slowly becoming one of costly support.

The history of ethical thought reveals many instances of the difficulty ancient institutions find in making changes in their moral practice, especially in the light of readings of ancient texts in the Bible and the Quran. Thanks to Roy Jenkins, as Home Secretary, the civil laws on divorce, homosexuality and theatre censorship were reformed in 1967 and 1968. The human rights of women and gay people were safeguarded after long and hard-fought battles in Parliament.

As this book reveals, toleration and sensitive care is now more often the custom in the Church for couples experiencing divorce, and slowly the attitude towards female ministry within the churches is changing, but this is not yet universal. Unfortunately there are still some who discountenance the remarriage of the divorced.

Archbishop Rowan Williams, commending a book entitled *Faith Beyond Resentment*, remarked: 'The very best theological books leave you with the feeling that perhaps it's time you became a Christian.' Many readers will find moments in this book on relationships that puts this challenging question to them. Sometimes divorce, with all its suffering, can be a good and brave decision. Sometimes it is the only way to accept the Gospel of Love and to live with merciful integrity with your nearest and dearest.

Here is a wise work drawing on the scriptures, poetry and deep personal suffering, all with a movingly expressed faith in God, the Lord Jesus Christ and the Hidden Spirit. Our author is widely read and has a happy and fulfilled second marriage. Many have written on divorce, but none from this particular angle.

Alan Webster

And Yet . . .

Even in the 'dead' darkness of winter
There are shafts of light –
Sunshine sparkling on frosty grass
Skeletal trees reflected on water
Muffled muted beauty of morning fog
Holly berries and robin's breast
A long evening of fireside and music.

Even in the depths of desolation
There are shafts of hope –
A kind word a thoughtful action
Revelation in the midst of struggle
The cathartic expression of pain
Through words, music, paint
Gifts of the Spirit
Hidden, secret, straining to burst out
Into new opportunity
As the hidden seeds in the winter earth.

Trust that, as the seasons,
The pain and destruction will pass
Will be transformed each time
Into something new and creative
Something richer for the experience.
Pain will return for sure
As winter follows autumn
But then will spring come again.
And even in winter
We must seek the shafts of light
And trust the seeds unseen but waiting
To grow and transform
Beneath the ground.

And our final season on earth?
We cannot know
But can only trust in God's grace
That then too shall we be transformed
Into something new and beautiful
Or we shall rest in the ultimate peace.

Introduction

Since my marriage broke up I have wondered how many people have been affected from a religious viewpoint as a result of the break-up of their marriages. For most of my life I was a Christian. Once upon a time I was inside the Church looking outwards. I could never understand people who had no faith, neither could I ever have comprehended myself in such a situation ... Maybe it is the 'Dark Night of the Soul'; maybe it isn't. Perhaps time will tell.

(A Broken Rites member in *The Rite Lines*)

*

This resource book was written not by an academic, theologian or philosopher, but by an ordinary person who has survived marriage breakdown and divorce. The views expressed are personal, borne of my own experience and that of many other Christians. The book has developed a somewhat feminine flavour because most of the contributors are women. I hope this will not deter men – even those reluctant to show their emotions, who face the world with a stiff upper lip – from reading it and finding help and comfort in their situation. Everyone, male and female (remember the man who in 2003 caused chaos in London as he campaigned on a crane for the right to see his child?), is hurt and damaged by the breakdown of their marriage and family life.

Some views expressed may, on the face of it, appear to be at odds with traditional biblical teaching; but this book is about living a Christian life and, at the same time, acknowledging our humanity and failings. God forgives us countless times; He wants only the best for us.

I offer no step-by-step instructions for surviving marriage breakdown and divorce; instead, it is hoped that sharing what we have learned will lead to a reaffirmation of God's love for you, your love of yourself and an increase in your self-belief and self-worth. Wherever you are at this moment in the journey back to life following the collapse of your marriage, be reassured, we have been there too. We understand.

If someone in your family is involved in marriage breakdown, I hope it will give you renewed hope that things can work for good, even though they may look as black as can be at present.

Whatever your reasons for reading this book, I hope you will find it is one of hope for the future and for coming to terms with the past.

Over the last 50 years attitudes in society to marriage and divorce have changed a lot. Divorce is now more common, and that goes for Christian couples too. One hears comments that divorce is 'no big deal'; it is simply the untying of a knot, the ending of a legal contract. Another comment one sometimes hears today is, 'Divorce is too easy.' While that may be true of the legal process of divorce, it is certainly not true of the resulting emotions and spiritual turmoil that those who have lived through it know only too well. These emotions affect not only the couple themselves but also their families and friends.

For most Christians the possibility that their marriage could fall apart, that divorce could be contemplated, let alone happen, is almost literally beyond belief. But belief in the divine does not make *us* divine. We are creatures of the earth, with earthly passions and emotions. We live in a world of fickle fads and fancies, of cruelty as well as kindness, hate as well as love. Our faith does not protect us from bad things happening to us – but it should, and can, help us to cope with even the very worst that life can throw at us. For Christians, in the ending of a marriage, which was intended to be lifelong and whose vows were made in the presence of God, there is an added, spiritual, dimension.

During the final puzzling and painful days of my own marriage I said to my husband, 'If you die before I do and find out the reason for all this – will you come back and tell me?' Little did I know then that I would not have to wait that long. Within a few years God had pointed me in a new direction and I discovered a purpose for my life and a happiness I couldn't have dreamed of in those agonizing days.

However, a life after divorce that is both happy and fulfilling comes at a price, as will be seen in many of the experiences shared in this book. In spite of the changes taking place in society, most of us still believe that the best, most satisfactory way to live is as part of a couple; ideally a married couple. For reasons of procreation and survival of the species, the pairing instinct is very strong in all creatures. But our human concept of love, especially romantic love, separates us from other creatures. We have a whole range of different emotions for every situation, and divorce arouses practically every emotion you can think of in addition to spiritual turmoil. Our unhappiness affects our bodies too. Many divorced people experience physical ailments. I had two major operations in the first three years after my divorce and, although these may have become necessary anyway in time, I firmly believe my mental and emotional condition adversely affected my body.

I hope the fact that so many people have successfully passed through this trauma-filled and painful period to emerge healed and strengthened will be an encouragement and source of inspiration. When our trust in another human being has been destroyed, it is hard to trust anyone else. But by rebuilding our self-esteem, confidence and emotional stability and learning that it is possible to continue to trust in God, we can pick up the pieces and use them to build a new life. A practical reality, as many can testify.

*

I thank the many members of Broken Rites who have allowed me to share their, often harrowing, experiences. For reasons of anonymity and to avoid embarrassment, names have been changed or omitted.

My grateful thanks go also to Gill Murray and Sister Rita-Elizabeth SSB, for their advice and encouragement at the start of the project and for patiently offering comment on the draft; to Alan and Margaret Webster for their ongoing support and encouragement; and, last but by no means least, to my husband, Bob, for putting up with my absence upstairs at the computer and for his willingness to be a sounding board to my thinking aloud.

Pauline Druiff

1

Begin at the beginning

Wedding bells

Every book has to have a beginning, and although it may seem odd to start this one with a chapter about marriage, we need to understand the nature of the relationship and how and why it can be broken, in order to pick up the pieces and move forward.

It is only at our own wedding that we really know what emotions are swirling around in the bride and groom's heads. The modern phrase 'men are from Mars and women are from Venus' is another way of acknowledging that we are different. We feel differently about things, our perspective on life is different. So we are going to approach our wedding in different ways. If I described my own wedding you might find it largely similar to yours – if you are a woman. If you are a man you may have totally different memories. For instance, we women tend to weep at weddings – mostly because we are happy! The bride's mother may weep for the little girl who is now grown up; the groom's because she has lost her son to another woman. The fathers will not feel like that. The bride's father may feel a sense of loss akin to her mother's, but he will also be very proud of this young woman, so beautiful in her wedding dress, and anxious about 'handing her over' to another man. The groom's father may feel he wants to warn him about some of the 'pitfalls' in an 'older-and-wiser man' way. In an effort to hide their emotions, laddish behaviour on the part of the best man and the bridegroom's friends can get the better of them at weddings. The stickers on the groom's shoes saying 'HELP!', visible when he kneels at the chancel step; the raucous jokes; the decorating of the car and stuffing of confetti everywhere; all these disguise the fact that they take marriage extremely seriously – but won't show it! The girls, meanwhile, are quietly dabbing their eyes and thinking how lovely the bride looks and, mistily, how romantic it all is; perhaps not considering that this is the most important step anyone can take, promising to share one's life with another human being – until death.

The fact is that men and women enter marriage with different expectations. These two sets of expectations can only blend if the couple talk about them and work at building a marriage that is a mix of what both of them hope for and expect.

*

You may be able to relate to this description of a 'typical' wedding – from the bride's point of view, naturally:

So there I was, all dressed up, flutterings in the tummy, nervously walking around the lounge while my father paced the hall, waiting for the car to arrive. After what felt like an eternity it drew up outside – right on the dot. Neighbours and passers-by wished me good luck before we were in the car and away. About halfway to the church my father said, 'Are you absolutely sure you want to go through with this?' I was startled; what a time to ask such a question! 'Of course I do,' I said. He went on: 'You don't have to. Don't worry about all the people waiting in church, the reception or anything. All that matters is that you are doing what you really want.' It was sweet and considerate of him, but I was adamant. I knew what I was doing.

So everything went as planned; the white wedding, the vows exchanged, the photographs (smiling until my face was stiff), the reception, the 'going away' to a great send-off.

The wedding service with its old-fashioned language was beautiful. It felt right and natural then to be 'given away' by my father. Nowadays I see it as something archaic. He didn't 'own' me, I was old enough to give myself. It also seemed right at the time to promise to 'obey'; but I wonder how many of us really believed that we would be expected to obey our husband? It didn't occur to me that a situation might arise when he would give me 'orders'. The vows appeal to many brides' sense of drama and youthful idealism. I pictured myself sticking to him through thick and thin, through sickness and poverty – and whatever other disasters might occur. The possibility of these things happening seemed extremely remote as I stood in church that day.

Of course, the wedding is not actually the beginning. That was some time before, in that heart-thumping, tummy-churning, dry-mouthed time when all one could see was the other person; when the slightest brush of hand against hand caused an almost electric shock.

By the time we reach the wedding day the hassle of the past few months and family feuds about who to invite and who to leave out are forgotten in last-minute panics about hair, dress, shoes and something blue. Nervous bride and proud father walk slowly down the aisle to join the anxious groom. The fairy-tale wedding you've always dreamed of is about to happen.

Afterwards, on a wave of euphoria, all doubts dispelled, you both know this marriage was made in heaven. God's blessing is assured. It is a union 'till death do us part'. The bride and groom set out on life's journey together with high hopes, waved off by happy family members and friends. Lots of prayers and good wishes. Yes, it was a great day.

Many of us at the start of our marriage are 'innocents abroad', believing that love and trust are all we need. We pick up our suitcases and leave for our honeymoon, unaware of the old 'baggage' we are taking with us. That unseen suitcase contains the sum total of our experience to date, our childhood and the observation of our own parents' marriage, or perhaps of life with a single parent, or life in an institution. Whatever our experience, it will have coloured our attitudes as adults and affected our relationships with others, especially with someone as close as a spouse.

The reality

> It was still dark when she rose at 6 a.m. to riddle and clear
> out the boiler. As she refilled it with anthracite and opened
> the blower to get it going again she thought of the two sleep-
> ing upstairs. Next she cleaned their two pairs of shoes – her
> husband's and her daughter's. Then she made his breakfast,
> just as he liked it, cutting his grapefruit and even buttering
> and marmalading his toast. She called up the stairs – 'Time to
> get up. When Dad's finished in the bathroom, you go in,
> Pauline. You don't want to be late for school.'

Sounds like something out of a historical novel, doesn't it? But
as recently as the middle of the twentieth century that is the way
it was for my mother and many women. Contrast that with
today's early-morning family (everyone milling around, getting
their own breakfast to cries of 'Get out of my way', 'I can't find
my football boots', etc.) and you begin to understand why life
now is more stressful than it was then. Even though previous
generations of women worked very hard physically in the home,
life was much less rushed than mine was as a young wife with a
full-time job a generation on from my mother's. As a young
married couple both working at the dawn of 'women's lib', we
shared many household tasks which my father and his contem-
poraries considered strictly 'women's work'.

From observation of my daughter's and other young families,
it is plain that family life today is even more different. Many
wives now have careers or responsible and stressful jobs, some
are family breadwinners, and some husbands are extremely com-
petent and willing to share child-minding, nappy-changing and
other jobs around the home. Complete role reversal, with mother
out at work and father working or just being at home 'mother-
ing', is not uncommon. Family life has changed a lot in the last
forty or fifty years, but increasing social and financial pressures
add to the strain on relationships between husbands and wives.

So although modern life has much to offer, our perfect marriage has come to grief in this new fast-food, instant world. Credit

cards, mobile phones, the internet, email and other modern technology tell us that not only can we have it all now, but that it is ours by right. We should all be very happy. So why aren't we? The 'instant-ness' of modern life has seduced us into wanting things that are not important and we have lost sight of many things that are. The life we envisaged on our wedding day has vanished. Let's take a look at some of the things that can go wrong in a marriage.

Growing apart

Growing apart is an insidious creeping disease. It is a dis-ease with ourselves, our lifestyle, our work, our partner, our home. At first it may affect only one part of our life, but unchecked it will spread until it envelops everything. As we grow older we change and mature, all the time continuing to learn. Learning brings knowledge; that, in turn, affects and often changes our outlook, our ideas and what we want from life. These changes need not cause problems if married people are able to share their views and ideas. They will not always agree, but communication allows them to understand each other and to appreciate, encourage and allow their partner's growth.

Couples who are unable to share their ideas, aspirations and new knowledge may find that the changes taking place in them will cause a rift; they will grow apart. The close understanding they once had has gone from their relationship. Unshared interests and hobbies have developed. More time is spent in the company of other people than with each other.

Conversely, human beings can also grow apart because they live 'in each other's pockets'. To be with someone too much can cause a relationship to go stale. Old proverbs come to mind – 'Familiarity breeds contempt' and 'Out of sight, out of mind'. These old sayings illustrate both of these extremes. When the balance of a relationship is lost, it becomes wobbly. Growing apart is the sign of a wobbly relationship.

Jonathan was shocked to discover his relationship was wobbly. He explained, 'My wife says our marriage is over, she won't discuss it and she won't come with me for marriage counselling.'

At the start of their marriage they would have thought it impossible that the day would come when she would say this and not even be prepared to go for help. No wonder he was in a state of shock. To live with someone and not know what they are planning or deciding is frightening. They had grown so far apart that communication had become practically non-existent. A case of 'less is more'? Less communication = more growing apart.

Desertion

By the time desertion occurs things have really reached rock bottom, though the final act of desertion can be a long time coming. Because most of us will have invested a lot of effort in a relationship before abandoning it, a person needs to be very unhappy to leave. Make no mistake, it is not as easy an option as might be imagined.

Some people will tell their partner why they are leaving, but many will not. Either way, the deserted partner will have difficulty with feelings of rejection. Although the reason may be hard to take, it is easier to come to terms with something you know than with something you don't. To be left in the dark allows the imagination to run riot. 'It must be something I've done which made him/her go.' Self-reproach may be inevitable – but it has to be grown through, even though the reason for desertion may be unconnected with the deserted partner's behaviour.

There are instances where the deserter's state of mind causes them to leave. Depression, worry, fear of failure, debt, work stress – the list is endless. Then there's that perennial reason – adultery – which I will deal with in a minute.

Another reason for desertion may be that the deserter was earlier the victim of abuse, which is what I move on to now.

Abuse – physical and verbal

Physical abuse is a major cause of marriage breakdown and would, one imagines, be easy to spot from the outside. However, those who suffer abuse are often extremely clever at hiding it, offering plausible reasons for visible injuries. Many hide from even their closest family the fact that their partner physically abuses them. They are convinced that everything will 'come right' because they love each other. But there's good and bad love. Good love isn't just words or feelings, it's also a consistent package of actions which show mutual respect and caring. Good love feels stable and secure. Being together is comfortable, not threatening, invasive or controlling. Each partner can relax knowing they are wholly accepted for who they are. 'Bad' love will have the opposite effect.

Heather, a victim of abuse, wrote:

> The problems I faced were his infidelity, abuse – both physical and mental – and recurrent cycles of withdrawal from both me and the children. The outbursts of violence and verbal abuse led me to seek a separation after 15 years but he threatened to commit suicide and we attempted reconciliation. He no longer hit me, but turned our eldest daughter out of the home at 17 for a minor misdemeanour, hit our 13-year-old daughter for 'giving him cheek' and when she was 17 hit her on her head with his fist. She took two overdoses during this time and had help from a psychiatrist. I eventually told him if he hit our youngest daughter, 14 at that time, I would speak out against him. He ceased all contact with us and we divorced after two years' separation.

This terrible and heart-rending tale highlights what victims of abuse and their children can suffer. It is hard to believe that a person can behave in such a violent way unchecked for so long. An immediate reaction to Heather's story may be, 'Why did she put up with it for all those years?' Many victims of abuse are willing to overlook or forgive, time after time. They desperately want to believe assurances that it will not happen again – and go on believing, until the next time . . . and the next . . . and the next . . .

The signs of verbal abuse, on the other hand, are invisible. No bruises or scars. No broken bones. Another old adage, 'Sticks and stones will hurt my bones, but words can never hurt me', just does not ring true to me. Much psychological damage can be caused by verbal abuse. A person's psyche and personality can be seriously harmed.

To be constantly 'put down', criticized, belittled and sneered at by your partner, especially in front of others, is humiliating and degrading. Such abuse wears a person down until they become a nervous wreck, unsure of their own capabilities, convinced of their own lack of intellect; they have become practically brainwashed into a state of self-disbelief. They are left without dignity and often, to crown it all, without a partner who, by now, has come to despise the person they married and is looking for, or has already found, a new relationship. Verbal abuse should not be underestimated as a cause of relationship breakdown. It is destructive in the extreme.

Adultery

Christians often consider adultery to be the gravest threat to a marriage. One wife wrote, 'My husband is a committed Christian and churchwarden. How could he go off with another woman?' Many churchgoers have a problem with sex. Almost everything else is forgivable, but sexual misdemeanour is portrayed by the Church as the worst possible sin. But God gave us our sexual nature – including our desire, passion and capacity for arousal. He must have intended us to use it and, I suggest, not only for the purposes of procreation but as described in the marriage service in the Anglican *Common Worship*: 'Marriage brings husband and wife together in the delight and tenderness of sexual union and joyful commitment.' Sex in itself is not sinful. Engaged in lovingly and sensitively it is a delight and a joy. Although the unfaithfulness of the partner is sinful, the fact that adultery is biblically condemned and breaks the vows made on marriage does not have to mean the end of a marriage. Many couples have come to terms with the adultery of one of the partners. Reconciliation, forgiveness and God's grace have enabled the marriage to survive and even be strengthened. But not every couple can cope with this problem. Laura wrote: 'I foolishly had a one-night stand when I was a young wife. I didn't tell my husband, believing that it was my problem, my guilt, and I shouldn't offload it on to him. He may have suspected, though, because 25 years later he accused me of unfaithfulness.' One has to have some sympathy for Laura, who bore her guilt for so long in order to save the marriage. Whether she was right or wrong, her adultery didn't need to destroy the marriage, which did eventually founder. The extent to which Laura's 'hidden secret', and subsequent alteration in her attitude to and behaviour in the relationship, contributed to the breakdown is something only the couple themselves will know.

Alcoholism

Alcoholism is an addiction and an illness that needs treatment. The first problem for many couples where one of them has become dependent on alcohol is that of acknowledging that there is a problem – the dependent spouse is in 'denial'. This can last for a long time. But whether it is acknowledged or not, the dependence will alter a person's capacity for emotional experience and reduce their ability to experience feelings such as empathy, curiosity, spiritual appreciation and deference. Conversely, stimulating emotions like pride and dominance will be over-emphasized. For a married couple, if one partner has become dependent on alcohol, the foundation of their relationship will be on emotional quicksand and whatever progress they may think they are making as a couple will probably come apart in the future.

Alcoholism untreated will result in other unhappy behaviour: violence, verbal and physical; withdrawal from a partner and family; and an unwillingness – often a subconscious defence mechanism – to avoid intimacy. They may be over-critical of others and sometimes become hypersensitive themselves.

All this resulting behaviour makes life with an alcoholic person very difficult. It seems that nothing one does is going to make any difference. And that is probably right, because the condition needs professional attention. However, such help cannot be made available until and unless the sufferer acknowledges their condition and asks for help.

If your marriage has broken down due to your partner's addiction (the above would apply pretty much to drug addiction, too), you will recognize the symptoms. That will not make it any easier to cope with, but may help you to come to terms with the fact that there may have been nothing you could have done. Except pray and hope that your spouse would seek professional help.

The partner of an alcoholic should not blame themselves. If you are still in a relationship with an alcoholic there are places you can go for help. Al-Anon provides excellent reading – leaflets and books – but the main thrust of their help is found in the family groups which provide support and a programme of recovery for families and friends of alcoholics. The wife or husband of an alcoholic may wonder why they need to 'recover' – they are not suffering from the disease. Al-Anon describes compulsive drinking as a 'family' disease because it affects the drinker's relationships – friendships, employment, childhood, parenthood, love affairs, marriages; all these suffer from the effects of alcoholism. A person who is very close to an alcoholic is most affected because those who *care* are the most involved in the behaviour of another person. The sensitive literature produced by Al-Anon, which follows the same 'Twelve Steps' as Alcoholics Anonymous (based on help from God – *as we understand Him*), is very helpful and well worth obtaining. Al-Anon is not allied to any sect or denomination. You will find their address, with others, at the end of the book under 'Helpful addresses' (p. 108).

Using religion to avoid intimacy

A Christian may use religion to avoid intimacy in an unhappy marriage, as Sara did. Sara was greatly valued in her local church. Her forte was welcoming new people and visiting them in their homes. She had a warm personality and many people were fond of her and grateful for her welcome.

Although some of the church community were aware that her marriage was unhappy, they did not connect that with her over-busy Christian activity. At home she could hardly bear to be in the same room as her husband who, though sensing that something was 'not right', was nevertheless unaware that their marriage was so near to collapse. Their children were grown up and had left home. Many factors, including the menopause and the 'empty nest syndrome', may have contributed to this situation, but ultimately it is another case of breakdown in communications. Eventually, after much prayer and heart-searching, Sara moved out and she and James later divorced.

This form of busying oneself is a trait that may be peculiar to Christians. Religion provides a conveniently legitimate reason to be out and about, visiting, going to meetings, to prayer groups, Bible study, home groups, missionary committees, all kinds of activities. When someone is constantly involved, as Sara was, alarm bells should start ringing in the church community.

*

Looking at these causes of marriage breakdown from a Christian point of view, are there lessons we can put to good use in our own situation? Perhaps we need to apply St Paul's description of love to our 'romantic' love, as well as our Christian love. He tells us in 1 Corinthians 13.4–7 (RSV):

> Love is patient and kind; love is not jealous or boastful; it is not arrogant or rude. Love does not insist on its own way; it is not irritable or resentful; it does not rejoice at wrong, but rejoices in the right. Love bears all things, believes all things, hopes all things, endures all things.

This is a good way in which to put our 'romantic' married love into action and, if we are coping with marriage breakdown and divorce, our love for our neighbours – including our former partner.

There is a strand running through these reasons for marriage breakdown. Lack of communication. Countless relationships founder because people don't talk to each other. There may be a lot of chatter on a superficial level – what the football team have done or we've run out of milk – but real talk is often non-existent. Lots of people are bad at expressing their emotions and even worse at examining their own motives. But this needs to be done in marriage; otherwise we become like the couple where the husband was shocked to find he had a wobbly marriage, because he didn't know what his wife was feeling or thinking.

The two key words in this chapter, put together, create the phrase 'loving communication' – so vital in any close relationship. It includes such mundane things as saying 'please' and 'thank you'. Making requests, not demands. Treating everyone, including children, with respect. In so many homes it is a 'free-for-all/survival-of-the-fittest/weakest-to-the-wall' situation. 'Thank you' doesn't take long to say but goes a long way to keeping a relationship on the right lines.

If, as I suggest, our former partner is now our 'neighbour', even though we may not like our former spouse we need to see that person as Jesus sees them. At the time of my own marriage breakdown and divorce I read a book written by the sister of former US President Jimmy Carter. In her book Ruth Carter Stapleton suggested this mental exercise: picture the person with whom you are in conflict, then picture Jesus standing with them smiling lovingly, part of the threesome. Holding this image in your mind, allow Jesus to speak to you.

Including God in my situation, allowing Him to take control and His love to enter the conflict, worked for me.

*

Make time for stillness and quiet –
to listen to the Spirit –
who makes everything new.

2

What is 'Christian marriage' – is there any such thing?

Wives, submit to your husbands as to the Lord. For the husband is the head of the wife as Christ is the head of the church, his body, of which he is the Saviour. Now as the church submits to Christ, so also wives should submit to their husbands in everything.

Husbands, love your wives, just as Christ loved the church and gave himself up for her to make her holy, cleansing her by the washing with water through the word, and to present her to himself as a radiant church, without stain or wrinkle or any other blemish; but holy and blameless. In this same way, husbands ought to love their wives as their own bodies. He who loves his wife loves himself. After all, no-one ever hated his own body, but he feeds and cares for it, just as Christ does the church – for we are members of his body. 'For this reason a man will leave his father and mother and be united to his wife, and the two will become one flesh.' This is a profound mystery – but I am talking about Christ and the church. However, each one of you must also love his wife as he loves himself, and the wife must respect her husband.

(Ephesians 5.22–33, NIV)

This one passage is sometimes regarded as a blueprint for 'Christian marriage'. But we humans can be inclined to use scripture for our own ends, justifying our actions and beliefs by quoting it out of context, without thinking about what God might be saying to us in a particular passage. We can personalize it to such an extent that it becomes an adjunct to our own thinking and behaviour, adopting a 'pick and mix' mentality – accepting what we like and discarding what we don't. We look at Bible passages in a narrow way, confining ourselves to a verse here and a verse there, without considering the context, social and spiritual, in which it was written.

If, as we believe, God values us all, men and women, equally, He surely does not expect us to dominate one another. The passage in Ephesians chapter 5, quoted above, is often interpreted as meaning that husbands can 'lord it' over their wives, who are expected to be obedient to the point of subservience. But it is not as cut and dried as that. We can also see that the demands on the husband are great – to love his wife as much as Christ loves the Church and to be willing to lay down his life for her. In return she is not to be subservient but to love, honour and respect her husband.

These two ways of interpreting St Paul's words are conflicting and often puzzling to Christians trying to live as Jesus taught. Jesus' message was about love, and the situation described by St Paul, in the first interpretation, appears to leave love out. The second interpretation includes it but in a much more chaste and high-minded way than the sort of earthy love which has always been part of human experience.

So what are we to make of this? Here we have only one of many examples of different interpretations of a piece of scripture. If we just read into scripture what we want, how do we arrive at what God wants?

Christians did not invent marriage. Unions between men and women have been taking place since human beings walked the earth. It was a way of life to which humans were led by their natural instincts. The story in Genesis of Adam and Eve adds God to the relationship, giving it a divine dimension. Adam and Eve were not Christian and the Garden of Eden story was addressed to the people of Israel and affirmed what they were already doing, making it something special by the introduction of God into the equation. It declared the union between man and woman acceptable and right because they were created to complement each other. In common with many other creatures, their union was partly to ensure the survival of the species.

Jesus, although comparatively silent on the matter of divorce, commends marriage, as a contract between two people for life. St Paul also commends marriage but, possibly rather dubiously, as a remedy for sin and to prevent promiscuous and indiscriminate sex. His view was presumably coloured by his belief that the end of the world was imminent and marriage would soon become irrelevant anyway.

In the early centuries of the Church's existence, marriage was not regarded as a sacramental rite but rather as part of the natural order of life. When it was realized that the Church needed to incorporate the natural order into its sacramental life, marriage became part of the institutional Church. Later, when social and Christian institutions became closely linked, it was felt that marriage should be regarded as permanent. The Church considered it sacred and compared the marriage relationship to the relationship of Christ with the Church. Marriage bonds could not be broken in case the divine union between God and man was damaged.

Every marriage is different, so there will be nearly as many opinions about what 'Christian marriage' is as there are Christian married couples. Marriage today is seen more in terms of a relationship than a practical arrangement to ensure the survival of the species and financial and domestic security, protection of lines of inheritance and other business-like matters. The relationship between the two people is paramount. It is assumed that if that is kept in good repair, everything else will follow in the natural course of events.

Modern couples usually get married as a result of 'romantic love' – the tummy-churning experience called 'falling in love'! When falling in love leads to something deeper and more lasting, then marriage may be seen as the logical step. Which is how we find ourselves in a church, a register office or, for some couples nowadays, even underwater or in a theme park, making promises to each other which are intended to last for life.

Let us consider two couples who have moved through the

falling in love stage and are now happily married. One couple are Christian, the other humanist. The Christian couple will consider their happy marriage to be a 'means of grace', a channel through which God effectively communicates His grace to them and others. The non-Christian humanists, who have no wish for, or experience of, a divine dimension in their very happy marriage, may nevertheless have a similar vision of what their mutual love can achieve in their own lives and the lives of others. Either way they are both upholding the 'sanctity' of their relationship, whether they believe it to be a gift of God or a straightforward covenant between them. The difference seems to be partly in the use of the words 'grace' and 'love', together with the Christian couple's belief that God is with them and has blessed their union.

The way in which God enters a marriage between Christian people is put in beautiful, easy to understand language in the introduction to the marriage service in *Common Worship*, now in use in the Church of England.

Marriage is a gift of God in creation
Through which husband and wife may know the grace of
   God.
It is given that as a man and woman grow together in
   love and trust,
They shall be united with one another in heart, body and
   mind,
As Christ is united with his bride, the Church.

The gift of marriage brings husband and wife together
In the delight and tenderness of sexual union
And joyful commitment to the end of their lives.
It is given as the foundation of family life
In which children are born and nurtured
And in which each member of the family, in good times
   and in bad,
May find strength, companionship and comfort,
And grow to maturity in love.

Marriage is a way of life made holy by God,
And blessed by the presence of our Lord Jesus Christ
With those celebrating a wedding at Cana in Galilee.
Marriage is a sign of unity and loyalty which all should
    uphold and honour.
It enriches society and strengthens community.
No one should enter into it lightly or selfishly
But reverently and responsibly in the sight of almighty
    God.

The first section tells us that marriage is a gift of God; He will honour it with His grace. Marriage enables a man and woman to grow together in love and trust and to be fully united, spiritually, emotionally and physically. Marriage is compared to the union of Christ with the Church. From a scriptural base, the Church 'owns' and sets out what a Christian marriage should be.

The second part is concerned with what was originally considered to be the most important reason for marriage – that children shall be born. Here, however, before mention is made of children, it is emphasized that the couple's sexual union should be one of delight, tenderness and joyful commitment. The Church has moved into the twenty-first century and acknowledged that sexual intimacy between a husband and wife does not have to be solely for the purpose of conceiving a child. It is also something the couple are 'allowed' to enjoy as an expression of their mutual love and affection. This is a huge step forward in the Church's attitude to human relationships.

Allowance seems to have been made here for people like me who find, after they are married, that they are unable to conceive and bear children, or who already know that they are unable to have children. Some of them will have difficulty coming to terms with what could be seen as failure, or entering a 'Christian marriage' under 'false pretences'. As an adoptive mother I find the word 'nurture' a great comfort. My son and daughter, now adult, have always been a great source of pride and joy to me.

Moving to the third part, this is a re-write of a section of the Book of Common Prayer introduction, in language more easily understandable to us in the twenty-first century. It still links modern marriage with marriage in biblical times, through the presence of Jesus at the wedding in Cana. The value of marriage in society is emphasized, while cautioning that it is not to be undertaken frivolously or for selfish reasons.

All of this is a great description of marriage for Christians. Hopefully churches are moving towards a vision of marriage that is in tune with, but not bowing to, modern life. For instance, the 'one flesh' statement has, over the centuries, come to be seen mainly as sexual union, but it is much more than that. The union of marriage makes the two people into one single unit. They do not have to think and behave in exactly the same manner, but effort needs to go into making sure that everything they say and do is agreeable to them both. Differences of opinion need to be discussed and those differences acknowledged and resolved or accepted. When I was a child it was still the norm for a wife to vote as her husband did. It would be difficult today for a husband to insist that his wife voted for the same party as he does; most women consider that it is only right they should think for themselves and make decisions accordingly. The days when women were looked upon as men's chattels are long gone, and I think Jesus would thoroughly approve of that!

So that is what people are signing up to when they marry in church. Christians marrying according to the customs of the Church can be assumed to be making a Christian marriage. But are they? The vows are only the beginning – the making of the marriage is in the day-to-day living out of those vows, the caring and the sharing, the loving, the quarrelling and the making up. Everything in their joint (joined) lives goes into the making of the marriage; but one extra thing can make it a 'Christian marriage' – their invitation to God to be a part of their whole life together. Humanists, and men and women of other faiths or of none, have just as great a capacity for human love as Christians have; they can and do make happy and lasting marriages. But all of us, Christians included, make mistakes and wrong judgements, and wander and away from our promises. No one is immune from temptation and sometimes it becomes impossible to resist, which is why marriages, even Christian ones, can come to grief.

Does the Bible help?

Most of the time, yes, but because, as we have seen, interpretations of biblical passages can be confusingly different, it is hard to be categorical about what makes a marriage specifically Christian. Interpreting the meaning of the Ephesians 5 passage as that the man should 'rule' the household and the wife submit, has led to many instances of severe maltreatment of wives in the belief that such behaviour is biblically commended. An example of this reached me in a letter from someone who had married a Christian, yet her experience of marriage with him did not correspond with what most of us would think of as being 'Christian marriage'. She told me she has had a strong personal and educated faith since she was 19. During training as a missionary teacher at an Anglican women's college she met her future husband, an ordinand at a nearby theological college. Their plans to marry caused concern because of extreme differences in their churchmanship. That in itself should be no problem, but a person's churchmanship will be reflected in their approach to other areas of life. For this couple it meant quite different approaches to almost everything. Her husband was not very accepting of women's ministry, which is surprising since he knew about her training when they met. Later, as an incumbent, he would not allow her to preach in 'his' church, which caused her great distress.

There are men who find strong, intelligent, outspoken women a threat. Perhaps he was such a man; I don't know. Anyway, it seems to me that the marriage, although ostensibly Christian, was doomed from the start. Their differences in churchmanship and biblical interpretation and teaching probably meant they were temperamentally and intellectually unsuited to the closeness of a marriage relationship.

Now divorced, these two have become good friends, because

there is space between them and they have lives independent of each other. She comments that the decision to leave him which she finally made was due to her Christian faith. Because God really does want the best for us and is with us in our heart-breaking situation, I believe He will bless the ending of a marriage between Christians, which may have been wrong in the first place.

Another wife says she thought she had a Christian relationship: 'I honoured my husband as head of the family, to take the lead in decision-making, and was very happy making life nice for him and the children. Now he tells me he doesn't love me.' What a devastating blow for a woman who believed wholeheartedly that she was living her married life according to God's will. The feeling when you think you are doing something right, only to be shown brutally that everything is apparently wrong, is so hurtful. It would not be in the least surprising if she has forsaken God and the Church altogether. In Christian marriage, as in any other, communication between the couple is vital – as vital as their communication with God. If her husband had spoken of his dissatisfaction they might have been able to sort things out. The marriage could have become stronger. Instead of which she is left with rejection and a sense of failure.

What do we tell the children if it goes wrong?

Telling children about marriage breakdown is difficult – compounded if both parents and children are Christian. Our children's expectations spring from what we have taught them about marriage. If a breakdown occurs we need to be able to express to them, if we have not already done so, what behaviour is acceptable in a marriage and what is not; whether according to our Christian values Daddy's or Mummy's behaviour is acceptable or unacceptable. Children do not expect us to break promises, to hurt others or to behave badly, yet here we are about to smash their world to bits. My own children were teenagers when the family split happened. I do not know even now the extent of their distress, but my son's reaction when told, alluding to his adoption, was to cry out, 'But you promised to look after me!' My daughter's reaction was, 'Why didn't you say something – I could have helped.' Both these comments cut me to the quick and are an indication of the hurt they too were feeling.

There is never a 'right' time to tell anyone bad news, but during my involvement with members and potential members of Broken Rites, one thing I always tried to get across was that you must tell the children. To acknowledge one's faults and failings to one's children is not easy. But, believe me, told sensitively and lovingly, they will not judge; in spite of their own distress, anger and bewilderment, they will be reluctant to apportion blame.

We need to remember that children are still children. They are fellow victims in the breakdown of the marriage and theirs is a particularly isolated pain. As comforting as it may be to a mother to find her young son attempting to 'take Daddy's place', she should not encourage it. It is important that children be encouraged to stay children and not assume 'adult' roles in the family. A 10-year-old may make huge efforts to be 'Dad' or 'Mum' when left without one, but their turn to shoulder this role and responsibility is still many years ahead of them. A young boy will feel the absence of a male figure in his daily life, a new area to learn to live with, and small children will need a lot of extra loving at this time. There will also be confusion in their minds because they will see the parent with whom they live as the one who deals with the day-to-day chores – the boring nitty-gritty of life – and the other one as the provider of the excitement of weekend treats and presents. Adults have a lot of responsibility in trying to keep the situation as 'normal' as possible in what is a strange and puzzling situation.

Some children experience guilt over their parents' marriage breakdown. They blame themselves; they ask, 'What have I done?' It is important to reassure them, whatever their age, that it is not their fault, they have nothing to blame themselves for. It is also important to ensure that, if possible, slanging matches between the parents do not occur within earshot of the children, and that neither parent 'slags off' the other to them.

What about sex?

Sex has always been a hang-up for Christians. Church communities often prefer to pretend it is something which Christian people 'don't do'. The truth is, of course, that pretty well everyone does. Until recent times, it was considered not nice to talk about or admit to having sex, let alone liking it!

But times change and now the pendulum has swung almost to the other extreme: on TV we are faced with people having intimate relations *in the corner of our sitting room!* In today's world, sex has become a leisure activity, like playing sport or going out for a meal.

So what about sex in our marriage? We have seen in the introduction to the *Common Worship* marriage service that it is to be tender and loving and that we can have pleasure in it. So Christians do not have to pretend any more. It is all right to show our love for each other in this way – and take delight in it. The ideal is to be aimed at, but there are marriages where sexual activity is less than ideal.

Such a story is Alice's, another Christian wife with a Christian husband. Not many husbands have such persuasive powers as this one.

For most of the 16 years of their marriage he induced Alice to accept the idea of sharing him sexually with other women, persuading her that her ideas of love and marriage were narrow and possessive, whereas he had developed a divine capacity for love. In time one of these ladies decided to leave her husband and move into Alice and her husband's home with them and their children. This ménage lasted several months. Eventually, unsurprisingly, the marriage broke up.

This may be an extreme case (or possibly not?) but I hope and believe that in most marriages sex is an important part of the way in which husband and wife demonstrate their deep feelings for each other and their ever-growing closeness, physical and emotional.

Finally, there is the matter of sex before marriage and after a marriage has ended (due to either bereavement or divorce).

Most of today's young people would think it old-fashioned and stuffy to even contemplate not 'having sex' before marriage. For the Church and its members this causes something of a dilemma. Many faithful Christians will have adult children who do not subscribe to their parents' Christian standards. However, in a more open atmosphere I imagine quite a number of parents would admit that they had not followed Christian teaching when healthy young adults but, like many things which are 'outed' today, it was kept under wraps. The assumption has been made that Christians will not enter a sexual relationship until they are married. It may have been the Victorians in the nineteenth century who first decided this rule should be emphasized, at the same time tacitly agreeing that, should it be broken, nothing would be said. History reveals that many Victorians didn't marry until after the birth of the first child!

There may always have been an element of hypocrisy in the insistence on chastity before marriage. In any event it seems that many young couples marrying today are already 'sleeping', if not living, together. A senior churchman told me about his son and his girlfriend, living together, who had invited him and his wife to lunch. Asked how he felt about the situation he wisely expressed the view that young people today have a moral code, though this may differ from that of their parents.

Sexual relationships after the end of a marriage are another matter. One correspondent wrote: 'My husband left me suddenly and without warning – my unmet needs for physical intimacy are unbearable.' There are many men and women who feel this way when the sexual relationship has continued almost up to the day their partner left. They feel stranded; their need for the warmth and comfort of physical love and companionship is unmet and likely to remain so. It is almost impossible to advise anyone in this situation, because what is suggested – either by a Christian or for a Christian – as a possible remedy might appear to be condoning what is believed to be sinful. A friend told me that she found regular massage helpful, in a sensuous rather than sexual way. She found it comforting to have her body carefully and gently massaged. Humans have a great need for physical contact with other humans. Aromatherapy and reflexology may help, too.

When dealing with this problem we need to come to terms with our faith, what we actually believe and what we believe God wants for us. I don't imagine God would want a series of 'one-night stands' for anyone, but there may be occasions when a tender and close relationship may be what He wants us to have – there are many ways in which love and affection can be expressed without full sexual union.

The report *Something to Celebrate,* produced by a Working Party of the Anglican Board for Social Responsibility in 1995, received a somewhat harsh reception, possibly because it contained assessments which were critical of the Church and an honest evaluation of its failure in the past to address people's problems and needs realistically. The report maintained that the Church had conformed to a too narrow view of marriage and family life, speaking about families in sentimental or exclusive ways that do not connect with real life. It went on to state that the idea of mutual, equal relationships between men and women is rooted in the Christian gospel, but the Church has often failed to respect the integrity of people's struggles, leaving them feeling excluded. Some have encountered disapproval and downright rejection when turning to the Church for help, feeling that the Church seems to care more about the legal status of a relationship than its qualities or the growth of the people within it.

Considering that at the time the report was written half of all marriages were still taking place in churches, it is amazing that the Church should still have been so out of touch with life as it is actually lived. Indications are that some progress has been made towards a more realistic understanding of human relationships and sexuality since then, but there is still a long way to go. There is more about sexual orientation in Chapter 5.

*

So, is there such a thing as 'Christian marriage' or should it be described as 'a marriage of Christians'? Being a Christian is not just about saying one is a Christian, it is about living as a follower of Jesus Christ. The main thrust of Jesus' teaching was that love is paramount; we must love God and love our neighbour as ourselves. 'Romantic' love, which often leads to marriage, is a part of that love.

Getting married in church does not make a Christian marriage. The two people who marry make the marriage. They create the contract between them; they are responsible for their own relationship. It is not something that happens in some magical way on our wedding day; it may take a lifetime of love, care and compromise to achieve. To see an elderly couple celebrating their ruby, golden or diamond wedding anniversary is a wonderful and encouraging thing.

Finally, the prayer said by the priest over the new husband and wife as they kneel at the altar after their marriage says everything needful about marriage before God – a marriage of Christians. But 'Christian marriage'? The decision is yours.

*

Almighty God,
You send your Holy Spirit
To be the life and light of all your people.
Open the hearts of these your children
To the riches of His grace,
That they may bring forth the fruit of the Spirit
In love and joy and peace;
Through Jesus Christ, our Lord,
Amen.

3

Emotional turmoil

A review of a recent film described a family who arrive penniless in New York from Ireland as 'emotionally shipwrecked, dealing with loss'. This phrase leapt off the page at me – it so well describes how we are at the time of marriage breakdown and divorce. Our sense of loss takes over and, like the father in the film, we find our emotions too difficult and painful to deal with or, like the mother, we adopt a 'business as usual' attitude in order to just keep going. The loss with which this family are coping is the death of a child. Poignantly, the film is dedicated to the director's own dead son. Even if I don't get round to seeing the film, it has already made a big impact on me.

Looking back, I think at first I was like that mother – keeping going, filling my life with work and the concerns of others. I will never forget the morning that the Decree Absolute plopped through the letterbox on to the mat. It was a working day in the boarding school where I was a housemistress, and all through it, in spite of the many calls for my attention, my mind continually returned to the memory of opening that brown envelope and reading the official confirmation of what I already knew – my marriage was over. That evening as I went on the rounds of the dormitories one girl said to me, 'What a boring day; absolutely nothing happened!' I couldn't tell her that for me it had been one of the most momentous days of my life.

Lots of us write poetry at times of deep emotional conflict, in an attempt to make sense of it all. Sarah Thorley's poem 'Decree Absolute' is a work of raw emotion, a graphic description of how she felt on the day her marriage legally ended.

Decree Absolute

Finishing ending closing finalising dividing separating
  dismantling splitting gulf chasm final end.
The screaming splintering breaking fragmenting tearing
  apart dismembering disintegrating has all been done
  already.
Now it's the mechanical clinical legal formalising neutering
  neutralising – paperwork.

I sit alone in an anonymous garden square with autumn
  leaves falling around me.
And hear absently the noise of traffic, of people about
  their own business and stare at the empty concrete
  space in the middle of the garden.
An empty space like my heart.

I've walked, one foot in front of the other, not seeing,
  tears dripping unwiped down my face.
When I walked out of that huge Royal Court of Justice I
  was alone . . . and where to go?
St Clement Danes was across the road . . . I went in and
  sat down in the back pew.
God wasn't there.
At least I couldn't feel him or speak to him.
Where do the others go when they leave the court? Alone.
Some had relief and smiles on their faces.
Most were grey and anxious and smoking cigarette after
  cigarette.

It was terrible in there.
An hour and a half I'd waited.
Waited.
No one spoke to me.
The air was thick with smoke and anxiety and depression.
There weren't even enough seats.
My knees felt weak, but I had to stand against a pillar for
  half an hour.

My name on the list: a number:
I never wanted this I wanted to shout.
I don't want it now.

A nice round woman in white skirt and some legal black
    cloak patted my shoulder and asked my name.
Looked at the list. Checked the numbers.
Not long now, she said.
I wished I'd had someone with me. But perhaps not.

But where to go and hide and cry after I'd seen the judge?
Just on to the street where everyone stares curiously or
    pretends not to.
Not that I really noticed.
That's where a priest should be. A counsellor, a comforter.
I would have cried on a shoulder. Talked to a stranger.
Well, my footsteps mechanically brought me to this park.
At least I can weep tears here inconspicuously.

Eighteen years and six months ago to the day.
We were just married.
What an occasion. What hope and faith.
The beginning. The end is alone and depressing and in a
    way, easy.
No one knows about today.
Not like the beginning.

What is your religious persuasion?
Christian . . . I swear . . .
I can't remember what I swore but it was a tatty copy of
    the New Testament (she said).
The kindly judge went through the formal questions.
Yes. Yes. Yes. I said.
The clerk with an expressionless face, made notes.
I grant you care, custody and control . . .
The papers are folded up, tied with pink tape.
Next please.

Goodbye dear says the nice round woman. And out I
  walk through the smoke and buzz of voices.
It's over. I'm divorced.

© Sarah Thorley, 1991
(reproduced with permission)

The loss we feel at this time is so enormous we can hardly bear
it. Emotions are released that can surprise us with their intensity as they run riot. We go through the whole gamut, sometimes several times a day. In the middle of the night we wake up
and there are these emotions driving us nuts. What can we do?
First, we must take a good look at how we feel. Because our
emotions are out of control, different times, places and experiences will evoke different emotions, often jumbled up together.
All these emotions are natural and normal – don't punish yourself even more by thinking you shouldn't have them.

Writing in *The Rite Lines*, a member of Broken Rites said:

I had many what I called my 'miserable half hours', when I
used to sit in the bath with the taps turned on a little so that
my landlady would not hear me sobbing. A vulnerable,
emotionally hurt person needs to cry. Tears are part of the
healing process. At times of great distress you are entitled to
indulge in crying sessions and allow your emotions to work
their way out of you.

Oh, the tears. Even now, 25 years on, I remember crying huge
silent tears in the bath as my world fell apart. We have all had
different experiences, but many of our reactions are the same.
What a great comfort that is.

Hurt

Emotional hurt is hard to deal with and is the trigger to many
other emotions. It can be painful to the point of being physical.
Sometimes it is so hard to bear it manifests itself as a headache

or a stomach-ache. For those things there is always the option of taking a paracetamol. But there is no painkilling pill which will remove the emotional hurt. That will only fade with time and if we are patient with ourselves. One of the most important things we can learn in this period of recovery after marriage breakdown is to be gentle with ourselves. We are fragile creatures, emotionally bruised and battered. These wounds will not heal quickly and gentleness and patience are needed. In the same way that it is no good telling a person suffering from depression to 'pull yourself together', there is no point in telling ourselves to 'get over it'. We will get over it in time, but for now, nurse the hurts gently as you would a physical injury like a broken bone, encourage them to lessen and finally leave.

Anger

It is natural when we have lost something we valued to feel angry. Very angry. Not always sure where our anger is directed, we thrash about in this emotion, lashing out in unexpected directions and at unexpected times. Mostly we are angry with our former partner; some of our anger is with God, some with ourselves. Our anger is so mixed up we are unable to work out how to deal with it.

We all experience anger in different ways. In children anger flares up quickly and dies down just as fast. Some people stay like that all their lives. In others anger is slow-burning, taking a while to get going, but when it does refusing to go out and smouldering on and on.

From childhood we may have been taught that it is bad to be angry; we shouldn't be cross. I suppose anger is one of nature's ways of ensuring that we protect ourselves if we are attacked. If someone hits me, my anger makes me want to hit him back. As adults society teaches us that this is not always a good idea, which is why we still believe that anger is not good. But there are occasions when anger can galvanize us into righting wrongs when, without it, we might just sit around and wait for someone else to do something.

Anger is a human response to being hurt. When we suffer loss, whether of a partner, our home or income, or our handbag to a mugger, anger is a natural reaction. Left unchecked it could be dangerous but, as suggested above, it can be used as a force for good. Feeling angry about a situation can motivate us to take some constructive action to improve it. Maybe to lobby the local authority for housing, write letters of application for jobs, go to the police about the mugger. Many good things can come from anger used properly.

Guilt

Feeling guilty is unpleasant. Guilt gnaws at us; it causes us to shoulder blame that may not be ours. Some guilt is necessary in marriage breakdown. Older and wiser now, I don't go as far as to repeat a favourite phrase of my younger days, 'Six of one and half a dozen of the other'. But I still believe that many of us unwittingly fuel the fire of marriage breakdown, often by what we don't do more than by what we do. In the first chapter, I mentioned Laura who had lived with the guilt of her adultery for many years only to find her marriage finally broke down when her husband wished to marry someone else. My point then was that the adultery itself need not cause marriage breakdown. But more can be learned from this incident. Who knows what might have happened if she had confessed right away to her lapse? Her husband might, as she feared, have thrown her out. But he might have been able to forgive her and the marriage could have survived and become stronger. Nursing her guilty secret damaged their relationship and, she believes, contributed to the eventual breakdown. She now knows what a huge mistake it is to think that not speaking at all is less damaging than telling lies. In this case, saying nothing encouraged her to keep quiet about other, less important matters, which distorted the lines of communication between them, damaging the relationship beyond repair.

Hate

Christians are constantly exhorted to 'hate the sin but love the sinner'. In abstract terms it is easy to follow this rule but in close up and personal terms it is hard to hate only what has been done to us, but not the person who has done it. My own method of coping was to think of the person as someone more to be pitied than blamed. Human beings' behaviour is often impulsive, without thought for others; at other times it is deliberately cruel and calculated. Either way hating the perpetrator does not improve the situation and it damages us. The example I quoted earlier of picturing the person in your mind and then picturing Jesus alongside them can help here. Directing hate at God is unfair of us – He shows us love and that is how we respond to Him! We have forgotten that God loves the person we hate; if He can love that sinner, who are we to do otherwise – even though we may sometimes wish He did not love them?

Relief

Don't feel bad if your reaction is one of relief. It is hard to imagine, before things reach the splitting-up stage, that you might actually feel relief. Yes, Christians are supposed to be married for life. But sometimes life changes so much that for reasons of our own safety or mental health, or that of our children, it may be better to call it a day. A partner who is violent, verbally abusive or suffering from alcoholism or drug dependency is in need of professional help. If such a person is unwilling to seek help, a spouse may find it a relief to leave the marriage. The relationship will have become so destructive there is no chance of rebuilding it. Relief can be felt for many reasons. Like the other emotions – don't fight it. You are not alone.

Jealousy

Who does not feel jealous when their partner finds someone else? Only someone who has ceased to care, or an angel – one with wings! This is one of the most human emotions there is and also one of the most potentially self-destructive. There is nothing good to be said about jealousy; it eats away at the heart and mind of the jealous person, breeding resentment, and should be avoided if possible. I have no pat answers to the question 'How do I avoid being jealous?' and can only repeat what I have already said: be patient and handle yourself gently – this emotion will damage only you. St Paul's description of love (on p. 11) is helpful, if you can handle the concept that real love considers the other person above the self. That is the only way I know in which to combat this feeling. I am not proud of the fact that in the early days after my divorce when my daughter said to me, 'What would you do if you met M in the street?' I quickly replied, 'Hit her!' 'Getting one's own back' is rarely satisfactory. I hope I wouldn't have carried out that threat!

Bitterness

My experience is that most of the emotions already described, left unchecked, will lead to bitterness, another extremely self-destructive emotion. Bitterness will always damage the self and will not solve a problem or allow help from outside. It will fester and grow into something so destructive that those who succumb to bitterness end up alone and unhappy with their problem. If we do not wish to end up like this then we need to deal with bitterness in a positive fashion, otherwise it will overwhelm us and we will become sour. I said in an article some years ago, 'Who would choose to eat a lemon when there is a sweet juicy orange in the fruit bowl?' Bitterness is damaging to our personality as well as our physical appearance. A sour face is not attractive and appealing to others. If you don't think you are squishy enough to be an orange, you can always be a welcoming rosy apple!

Sense of failure

We all want to be winners. To fail in a relationship is one of the hardest things to come to terms with, and because marriage is so important we do not like to be seen to fail. Failure brings with it a sense of guilt. We have done something that has caused our marriage to fall apart, or perhaps we have failed to do something. Although divorce is now legally a 'no fault' procedure, it does not mean that we do not have some guilt for what has happened. We feel we are a failure as a person, resulting in low esteem and loss of self-confidence – which have been dealt with separately in Chapter 6, 'Who am I?' However, they are *not* separate. Every emotion we have during the collapse of our marriage and divorce is linked to all the others. It is the cumulative effect of all these emotions that increases our feeling of failure – creating the vicious circle from which it is so hard to break free.

The very fact of a marriage having taken place in church will add to the pressures on Christian people who have taken their vows seriously. One woman felt that God was displeased with her decision to divorce her husband and, consequently, with her as an individual. Our expectations of our marriage, that it will be happy, harmonious and for life, are rooted in our Christian heritage, as is how we feel about divorce.

But much of what has been said already here, coming from others who have survived the experience, will give hope to those who feel they are failures and of little worth. We know that being loved increases our self-confidence. We know that God loves us – He will not withhold that love or be displeased with us for failing. He may be saddened but He will be compassionate and caring, wanting us to build up our confidence again and feel proud of ourselves. God wants us to succeed in whatever lies ahead of us and to face it without shrinking, accepting that although what has happened may be bad, we can still turn things around and find good in a bad situation.

We need to adopt a positive approach to our new single status, looking for the advantages and not bewailing the disadvantages, reminding ourselves daily of the reality of God's love and care.

*

An associate member of Broken Rites whose marriage went through a very rocky patch related strongly to the way many divorced people feel and was able to express this in writing. I am glad she did, as it means I can share what she said with you:

> I feel for you all, and have suffered the long hours of loneliness, feelings of rejection, tears and headbashing as a result of frustration. Often I wanted God to be near me, to put His arms around me and comfort me . . . Every now and then I would have a wonderful experience of His love for me. Now, looking back, I see the pattern and how He has led me. I have suffered with you . . . walking the streets in tears, and I've been very upset with the pain you have suffered.
>
> (from *The Rite Lines*)

Happily, the marriage survived; the writer and her husband were able successfully to re-establish their relationship.

*

It is possible to deal positively with the very human emotions we feel as our marriage disintegrates, as shown by the following quote:

> Well – here's me – 21 years of marriage now behind me – at least that's where I keep trying to put it – it does slink back into nightmares, into cold sweats, into tossing early mornings. But – I am still me. Scarred – yes; scared – yes; older – of course; ready to start afresh – YES YOU BET. I've still got some 'get up and go', and maybe just enough time and energy to make a little more for me, after so much for others – for him – for the job . . . I feel a complete idiot for the years in

agony – the too close suicide, the anti-depressants and the
rest. But here I am – 3 fantastic kids, 2 dogs, 1.5 cats – one
moved and settled the other not quite – no settee and half a
canteen of cutlery . . . I am human, proud to be and with my
feet of clay to boot!

(A Broken Rites member, in *The Rite Lines*)

One can almost feel the hurt this person has lived through, but
she has emerged from it strong and with her sense of humour
intact. Like her, we are all only human and trying to cope with
everything on our own is too hard an option. We need to find
the way back to allowing God into our situation, for that is how
to overcome these overwhelming emotions that trouble us. A
good first step is to make time for quietly listening to what God
may be saying to us – He always has the answer, but we do need
to listen with our hearts in order to hear it.

Family matters

> *When separation or divorce occurs, it is not only*
> *a marriage break-up. It is a family revolution.*
> (Hannah Bell, *Pierced to the Heart*)

In the course of writing this book I have had the opportunity to
talk to people whose daughter or son has divorced or is experiencing difficulties in their marriage. When a marriage breaks
down it affects not only the couple themselves but also the
wider family. In particular, the parents of a divorcing son or
daughter will be suffering many emotions similar to those of
their child.

One lady, now 'single again', was deeply shocked when her
daughter phoned to tell her mother that her husband had
left.

I couldn't believe it. They had seemed so happy together, with
their three little boys. I felt as though I had been kicked in the
stomach. I didn't want her to go through all that I had been

through – the pain and anguish, the soul-searching, the guilt. I didn't want her children to grow up with Mum trying to be Dad as well. I didn't want her husband to have found a new model. I went to church the next day and wanted to stand at the back and howl out loud. It opened up all the old wounds and this time they were someone else's, someone dear to me.

I was moved and saddened to see this lady so distressed by what she regarded as a repeat of her own situation. She continued,

My own parents were dreadfully upset when my marriage broke down – I understand it now. The only thing you can do is to be there for your child, even if they can't talk about it to you – so often a very close friend is better for that. And be there for the grandchildren, who don't understand at all and can't articulate their feelings. You feel very helpless in the face of other people's misery, you wish you could do it for them, suffer for them. But in the end you stand alongside and encourage them as much as you can while they suffer and learn to cope. And you pray all the time, because God loves each one of them and has a life for each one to live, though it is obviously not according to our plans.

Another grandmother told me about the breakdown of her son's marriage. She had written about this soon after it happened. Hannah Bell (a pen name) wrote movingly in her book *Pierced to the Heart* about how she and her husband felt when their son and his wife divorced. Talking to Hannah today it is evident that, 20 years on, she still vividly recalls her feelings at that time. Their whole family are deeply committed Christians. Their son Ray's wife, Jean, was not, but was always willing to talk to Hannah about her faith and was supportive of Hannah's work for the church. It was a huge shock for Hannah and her husband when they discovered that Jean was having an affair and was expecting another man's child. Jean eventually moved out and a year later the divorce was made absolute. Hannah's emotions ran riot as much as Ray and Jean's will have done.

Initially she felt anger (at Jean), fear (for Ray's future and that of the three children), guilt (how much was she, Hannah, to blame?) and doubt (wondering if she was naïve to believe so ardently that prayer 'will make everything all right'). She asked the question, 'Why has God allowed this to happen to us?' These emotions and the question will be familiar to us all. And we thought we were the only one feeling like that!

Hannah reckoned it took them several years to work through various stages of trauma caused by the breakdown before they were able to face it. Further emotional crises occurred at times, such as when the children had difficulties which affected their health and schoolwork and when Ray decided to marry again. Parenthood and its attendant worries don't end when one's children become adult. Hannah learned that through it all her Christian faith was able to sustain her. Her book ends: 'Life is an ongoing journey, leading finally back to God. As I finish writing this I can only bow my head and say, *"Thank you, Father".*'

The other story I want to share with you comes from a lady whose daughter is experiencing difficulties in her marriage. There has been a long-drawn-out deterioration in the relationship and this mother feels completely helpless. She understands her daughter's problems, but also has affection for her son-in-law, and is at the same time desperately worried about what the situation is doing to her grandchildren. No one can know at present how it will be resolved, but her fears for the family are countered by a determination to stay focused and 'stand alongside', giving support to her daughter as she wrestles with her problems and to her grandchildren, always being careful to refrain from making judgements.

Although it is hard for other family members, none – even those who may themselves have been divorced – can truly know what the couple and their family are going through as their marriage crumbles and falls apart. For everyone concerned the wounds will gradually heal, but the scars will remain. That is how it is. In these circumstances we can only watch, hope and pray as Mary did at the Cross. She found comfort in later events, after the darkest hour had past. We can gain strength from the knowledge that our darkest hour, too, will pass, and look forward with hope to the future.

*

To end this chapter I would like to quote another Broken Rites member who shared her experiences in *The Rite Lines*. *The Rite Lines* is greatly valued by the members of Broken Rites. Many of us have found great help and comfort in the articles, comments and poems contained in it. For me it emphasizes how much is to be gained by sharing in a self-help group. There are such groups for separated and divorced people all over the country; some are mentioned at the end of the book, but local groups often advertise in public libraries – a good place to start when looking for helpful resources.

Emotional recovery after my husband left

- **My first recovery was RELIEF**
  Relief from the public image, dealing with the anxiety of living on the other side of an angina sufferer who had already had two heart by-passes and from trying to please and sidetrack the flare-ups that his fiery temperament deemed necessary to throw up.
- **Second recovery: regaining my sense of fun**
  So a Laughter Course run by Robert Holden was followed by a Happiness Course shown on TV's QED programme.
- **Third recovery: trying to understand the anger**
  I encountered the then Quaker course of Alternatives to Violence Project. I felt violated and revenge was just around the corner. During the next few years I trained as a facilitator for AVP – a wonderful self-affirming course. Now I co-ordinate three courses a year and work with a team of facilitators in a prison for male prisoners. Nothing could have prepared me for my change of role, my degree of confidence and my understanding of the punitive side of my nature.

- **Fourth recovery: Quaker silence and healing**
  Plus meditation sessions in a friend's studio in a lovely lilac room with incense and candles burning.
- **Fifth recovery: adventure**
  South Africa – Lesotho – four trips to Italy, two trips to Spain and a month in Prague learning to teach English as a Foreign Language.
- **Sixth recovery: continuing music lessons**
  Ideas about joining a Jazz Course this year.
- **Seventh recovery: swimming**
  Three times a week at 7.30 a.m.

I'm now looking forward to the next five years with joy and thanksgiving, upheld by colleagues and friends and by the spirit within us all for well being.

*

Make time for stillness and quiet –
to listen to the Spirit –
who makes everything new.

4

Faith issues

'Where has God gone?' 'Why has God allowed this to happen to me?'

> I felt as if I was losing my faith. As I was working full time and running a busy household, I got up earlier and earlier to have a 'Quiet Time' praying and reading. Struggling, I experienced what was euphemistically termed 'a nervous breakdown', was hospitalized and invalided out of work.
>
> A year later we moved. 'A fresh start.' I began to go downhill again and was found a counsellor. It was another two years before I began to realize that the problem was not spiritual but marital, but it was too late. We separated. I was 50 years old. For five years I continued to struggle – to no avail. I could not cobble together a faith that worked any more – after a lifetime. Since then I have always kept open the doors, reading, listening, thinking. Attending church with two of my children, but only then. Nothing 'works'.
>
> (Denise, former clergy wife)

That sad and moving story is a graphic illustration of how marriage breakdown and divorce can affect not only our physical and emotional life, but our spiritual life too. Denise is half right in saying it was a marital and not a spiritual problem, but the marital problem *caused* the spiritual problem. The saddest part of all for Denise is that in spite of continuing to try to organize her life with time for reading, listening and thinking, she has not been able to rebuild her relationship with God. This chapter contains some suggestions for re-establishing that relationship; I hope they will be helpful. But first a bit about how, as Christians, we understand the marriage relationship.

First, we believe that marriage is for life. There is ample evidence and a firm basis for this belief in the Bible. Our personal interpretation of the scriptures will affect our response, but common to most Christians who divorce will be a deep sense of failure and inadequacy.

It has been suggested that one phrase in the marriage service may be a stumbling block to our understanding of failed marriage: 'Those whom God has joined together, let no man put asunder.' The words have a ring of censure about them. But consider them from a different angle. Two people marry each other. Although the priest conducts the service and God is present, it is they who are joining themselves together. The implication in the quoted phrase is that the union is God's will; He has decided that this particular couple should marry. Certainly they are joined 'in the sight of God', but supposing God was standing by to bless them, although not really happy about their union? Just because we believe, and the vicar says, that God is joining them together, He may not be. After all, not all marriages are 'made in heaven'. Should the marriage subsequently fail, can the couple reconcile reality with the ideal?

I believe the answer must be yes once we understand and deal with how we feel when we fall short of God's ideal. To be honest, we must all have fallen short on many other occasions and although this occasion is bigger than most we need to approach it in a similar way. We could start by answering the following questions, posed in Wendy Green's book *The Christian and Divorce*, p. 57.

1 *Can I forgive myself?*

For some this may the hardest to answer. To return to Laura, the lady who kept her adultery a secret for so long: for her, forgiving herself was difficult. Indeed, for many years she found it impossible. Believing that God had forgiven her was easy – she had no doubt that repentance had led to God's forgiveness. But she could not forgive herself. She had shouldered all the blame and the guilt (the fact that it takes two 'to tango' did not seem to affect that!), which made it impossible for her to move forward.

2 *Do I believe God forgives me?*

Laura had no problem believing this but did not fully understand what God's forgiveness meant until in a book by Corrie Ten Boom she came across a description of God taking our sin, forgiving it, dropping it into the deep water and then – this was the bit which expanded her understanding – putting up a sign: 'No Fishing'. Laura realized that all those years she had been *saying* she forgave herself only to regularly fish up the sin and have another look at it. She finally understood that to forgive oneself and then *leave it alone* is the key to finding the route to healing of the spirit. She commented, 'God is big enough to forgive anything for which we are sorry – are we so small-minded that we can't do the same?'

3 *Can I forgive others their faults?*

The answer to this becomes easier once we have grasped the concept of not trying to go one better than God. There may, of course, be the problem of not knowing whether the person concerned is repentant. I personally believe that to be irrelevant – forgiveness on our part is a sign of our Christian love and care and ultimately is likely to be of more benefit to us than to the person we forgive. This may sound selfish but the healing of only one of two people is good, even if healing both of them would be better. And we do not know how God is working in that person – He may use our forgiveness in ways we cannot imagine.

4 *Could I help someone else understand and accept God's forgiveness?*

Once you have experienced God's healing forgiveness for yourself it will be easier to help another person understand and accept it. It may take time and patience but with the grace of the

Spirit, as they see how forgiving has brought about healing in you, they will begin to understand and accept it themselves.

This is only the beginning, but if we can find answers within ourselves to these questions, much will become clearer and we will have started on a path leading to a new life.

So, we have a choice. Do we start a renewed search for that something beyond ourselves that we understand to be God, or do we find our comfort and solace in other things? Choosing the latter can lead to a wilderness where our own inner strengths diminish in direct relation to the frantic filling of every moment with 'busyness'.

Looking for help with spiritual struggles during my own divorce I was introduced to Glad Bryce, who had studied the spiritual dimension of divorce in depth, both academically and from her own experience. Glad, whose first marriage ended in a painful divorce, is a graduate of Hamilton Teachers College and the University of Toronto, Ontario, Canada. She has a good track record as a consultant in education and family life, and directed courses and seminars on being 'single again' for the Diocese of Toronto. Now widowed after a happy second marriage, Glad has four grown-up children and three grandchildren. Since 1982 when Glad wrote her book *Divorce and Spiritual Growth*, attitudes and regulations in the churches have altered and progressed, but that does not invalidate what she has written – it witnesses to the fact that many people have been able to demonstrate to the churches that divorce is not the ultimate sin; it is forgivable, as are all other sins. I can do no better than to include here some of what Glad had to say:

> Whenever a crisis happens in our lives, our spiritual relationship with God is challenged. We either turn toward God for inner strength and consolation or we turn *away* from him. During separation and divorce the loss of direction and accompanying disorientation create an added need for the strength of God's presence in our lives. If the turn toward God is taken, the potential for strengthening faith is

increased. It is in this way that spiritual growth through the divorce process happens.

The testing of your inner strengths, your own relationship with God, and your interpretation of your Church's theology are part of the spiritual aspect of divorce. Since divorce is a major crisis, it provides an opportunity to test your faith. The need to place your entire situation at God's feet will lead to new paths. Although the hurt and helplessness are over-whelming, God responds to you if you turn everything over to his keeping.

Trusting in God's healing power and in his ability to inter-vene in our lives may be the most difficult thing we have ever tried to do. I can remember very vividly making the decision to get away to the convent of the Sisters of Saint John the Divine in Willowdale, at the time of my separation, to sort out what had to be done. My sense of helplessness was com-plete. When I expressed this to a sister she said I must place everything at Jesus' feet; I must turn my life over to his care. As the retreat went on, I tried to direct all my thoughts to the foot of his altar. It was this conscious act of giving myself over to Jesus' keeping that assisted me in many of the mammoth tasks that were ahead.

At times, during the succeeding months and years, I had no idea of whether Jesus was guiding me or not. In recent years I have been able to see God's loving care in those years. At the time it did not seem evident. The test of faith was being able to trust in Jesus enough to let the pain continue without any apparent end being in sight. Perhaps this is the test of any-one's spiritual life, whether a crisis of divorce is being experi-enced or not.

Criticism is directed towards divorce as being one of the major factors in family breakdown. Divorce does not cause the breakdown – people do. When love between two people can no longer continue, it is necessary to deal with this fact in some specific way. If all assistance has been sought to help the relationship back to good health yet this has proved ineffec-tive, then I believe Christ would want the sin to cease.

Marriage needs to have two people committed to it. If one is unable to agree to make the marriage work, then it is impossible for the other partner to continue the marriage. Divorce allows a legal recognition of the fact that the marriage between two people is no longer functioning.

Because divorce forces us to assess our spiritual lives, the growth, which results, can help Christ to enter our daily existence. The hurts and wounds caused by a destructive relationship give Jesus a chance to enter in. The healing he brings is part of the Christian experience. He was sent by God to love. He showed us the way to become loving.

It seems to me unlikely that Jesus would speak in condemnatory terms of the breakdown of marriages that have become more destructive than constructive. He would, I am sure, speak to the social conditions of the twenty-first century just as He did in His own day. Can He really want us to remain in harmful relationships?

Glad continued:

While he upholds the perfect relationship, he calls us to recognise the truth in our lives. If the truth of life includes unhealthy relationships, which cannot be made sound again, then the Christian responsibility is to make changes. This could mean divorce. Jesus showed that we are rational beings able to make decisions and able to think for ourselves. He approves of us making sense of conflicting situations. If divorce is the only way to make sense of a marriage that has died, then he would not condemn.

The Christian experience of divorce includes the relationships within a parish. Because this varies so widely, it is difficult to speak directly to given situations. However, there are some general guidelines that can be applied. The relationship with the parish priest is often the most critical one. If there is an acceptance and empathy to the marriage breakdown, help will be forthcoming. Where this does not occur, other parishioners may fill the gap. At times the priest may be quite threatened by your situation and, for self-preservation, may remove himself from any active healing.

Some understanding of Glad's final comment may be found in Chapter 5, on clergy marriage. Clergy and their spouses are as human as the next person, as you will see from the response of Gina, a former clergy wife, when asked what the separation and divorce did to her faith/worship/spiritual life:

> Oh, it shot it out of the water, in a nutshell. The outward forms remained and there was a large amount of going through the motions. I think this was due to a desire to ensure some sort of consistency and familiarity in the midst of a turbulent sea with waves threatening to sink us all. The lovely picture language in Psalm 77.19 about a pathway through the sea that no one knew was there, and a friend telling me that the sea in Old Testament times was akin to chaos, helped . . . oh did that help. It helped in the very bad times when I wanted to curl up and let no one near me. It helped in the middle of the night when I knew I was alone. And it helped in church after the service, over coffee, having to listen to people talking and being totally unable to hold a conversation in my head. It helped because that's how I felt.

It is not hard to identify with that. I am happy to say that Gina has moved on and is getting on with her life. There is a lot to be said for what Gina calls 'going through the motions'. Persevering with the habit of regular worship and staying in the church family with which we have become familiar may not be easy, but it gives us a sense of 'normality' in what is, for us, an abnormal and unfamiliar situation. If we have moved away from familiar surroundings and need to find a new church, we must pluck up our courage to walk in and 'try it out'. It is important to be as sure as we can that the community and style of worship feel welcoming to us. When I moved to a new area I found a church I thought would suit me and quietly attended for several weeks sitting near the back and keeping a low profile. People were welcoming but not pushy, which I appreciated. I gradually became integrated, mixing with people at after-service coffee, getting to know them. Within a year I was voted on to the PCC and have been totally involved with my local church ever since. Not everyone would welcome so much involvement, but for me it was a life-saver. I needed to feel wanted and appreciated and so valued by God as well as by the folk around me. Spiritual dryness can be combatted by warm and loving care from a church community. How wonderful it would be if all congregations were able to be so welcoming and outgoing, without piety or 'in-your-face' pushiness.

A different view of the value of 'going through the motions' comes from Jane, another former clergy wife:

> I think I now realize that my church-going was a habit, and now that I am out of that routine I don't feel the need for it any longer. I still enjoy the odd service – particularly in a cathedral with wonderful music and incense where it becomes a theatrical performance, and I can appreciate that part of it – but I don't think I will ever return to being a regular member of any church community.
>
> As for my faith, who knows? Sometimes I think I believe – other times I am not at all sure. And for the spiritual life – I'm not even sure that I know what that means.

I feel sad that Jane seems to be saying that although she still has a belief in God it is not firm enough for her to put that belief into practice. Her church life did not apparently provide a home and a safe haven from the storm that erupted. However, she still occasionally enjoys the more theatrical type of worship. She has faith without commitment. Many people will identify with Jane: because we may think the Church has let us down, we think that God has let us down and we walk away from the faith commitment we had. Glad Bryce's belief that divorce can bring spiritual growth will sound like a fairy story to Jane. We don't know the reasons for Jane reacting in this way, but to share a little more of what Gina says may shed some light here:

Life was chaos. It didn't look good. It was a mess. It made a mess. It caused pain, distress, confusion, anger, retaliation, worry, sleepless nights, tears, illness and fury; and that was just for our friends and family.

Good grief. Objectivity. Oh how I lacked it, desired and required it. And how wonderful to have friends who absorbed the hurt and then wouldn't do it any more! How good to have friends who were able to still be there when I made those tentative steps back to sanity again.

Gina adds some points for moving on:

- Try to be patient, have hope and trust in God for the future, as He has helped amazingly in the past.
- Try to put yourself in others' shoes, e.g. fellow church members.
- Very often it is best to say nothing and let others work out the truth.

Spiritual direction

I would like to make an addition to Gina's suggestions for getting back in touch with God, prompted by a comment from those friends who 'then wouldn't do it any more'. They told her: 'You need to go and talk to someone outside the situation, you need to do it soon.' The person you need may be (don't be put off by the name) a spiritual director. Spiritual direction is an ancient ministry which is now regaining popularity. Many men and women, lay and ordained, are training to be spiritual directors. The training not only gives people skills for this ministry, but at the same time it deepens their own spirituality. The Revd John Twisleton in an article for the *Chichester Diocesan Magazine* describes spiritual direction as: 'a term used about a prayerful process in which people help one another to come closer to God. The traditional phrase "spiritual direction" is a rather uncomfortable term to modern ears and many prefer the term "spiritual companion" or "soul friend".'

Paradoxically, what a spiritual director does not do is direct, but such a person can be an enormous help in sorting out our personal belief system. Also, a spiritual director is not a counsellor. One spiritual director makes the following comparisons between the two functions:

A counsellor is concerned with encouraging	A spiritual director is concerned with encouraging
growth of the ego;	letting go of the ego;
self-assertiveness;	self-abandonment;
personal autonomy;	reliance on the Holy Spirit;
freedom from guilt;	repentance;
our past life conditioning our present behaviour;	the world to come conditioning our present behaviour;
seeing oneself in relationship to others;	seeing oneself in relationship to God;
viewing life as an opportunity;	living life to the glory of God;
personal well being.	salvation.

For me, spiritual direction was not only an invaluable resource in the rebuilding of my life after divorce but remains so in my spiritual life today.

The task of the spiritual director is to listen, and in so doing to give each person the opportunity to grasp their own experience, and to hear together both the reality and the challenge of the word of God at this particular moment to this particular person; to take the person where they are, not giving the impression of knowing the answer. If there is a 'solution' it will emerge from a prayerful listening and waiting on God together. The director's aim is not to judge or pry.

Here are some more quotes about spiritual direction:

Get yourself a good and faithful gardener; one who is knowledgeable about sowing and watering and watching and gathering the fruits of the garden.

(St Anthony of Florence, 1400)

The director's business is to go behind, and to watch God going before. He must keep his eye fixed on God, who is in the dimness ahead. He does not lead his penitents. The Holy Spirit leads them.

(Fr Faber, 1850)

What happiness, what joy, to have a person to whom you dare speak on terms of equality as to another self. You need have no fear to confess your failings to such a person.

(Aelred of Rievaulx, 1100)

I particularly like the second sentence of Aelred of Rievaulx's quote – 'You need have no fear to confess your failings . . .' When I first found a spiritual director it was like a weight lifted off my shoulders. I could speak of my failures, my laxness in prayer and Bible reading. It was so wonderful not to be judged and found wanting. I understood at last that I had to be (you'll be tired of hearing this) 'gentle with myself'. Instead of judging myself and feeling guilty for neglecting God, I need to tell Him I'm sorry and try harder. Making a regular time for being with Him once a day may not happen all the time, but the more we do it, the better we become at it. Just allow for the lapses – the times when you are interrupted by the telephone, or the man who has come to service the boiler. God understands all that. What He will not understand is why we should then stop altogether because we have missed a time or two!

To avoid embarrassment or awkwardness, spiritual directors do not generally work with people from their own church or area. If you think you would like to experience spiritual direction ask your minister or priest to help you find one.

That 'quiet time'

I was extremely cheered by reading the following Bible passage:

Very early in the morning, while it was still dark, Jesus got up, left the house and went off to a solitary place, where he prayed. Simon and his companions went to look for him, and when they found him, they exclaimed: 'Everyone is looking for you!' Jesus replied, 'Let us go somewhere else – to the nearby villages – so that I can preach there also. That is why I have come.'

(Mark 1.35–8, NIV)

It would seem that Jesus was suffering from a bout of insomnia. This will ring bells with many of us who lie awake in the early hours when everyone else is asleep. But instead of tossing and turning, huffing and puffing, should we, as He did, get up and make use of the time? The thought of Jesus, unnoticed, quietly creeping out of the house and going off to somewhere solitary is rather appealing.

However, it wasn't long before His quiet solitude was interrupted by His worried friends searching for Him. 'Everyone is looking for you!' they exclaimed. It must have been tempting to growl, 'So what? I'm having a quiet time on my own. Go away.' Instead He says, 'Let's go somewhere else,' and off they go on a teaching and preaching tour round the nearby villages. Could we but be so gracious to those who interrupt us when our quiet time is disturbed. Jesus showed remarkable patience and forbearance with His friends. He didn't snap at them but just accepted the interruption and turned, without rancour, to a different task.

The Christian life is one of reception and response to God's initiatives. Sometimes our comfortable relationship with God is so greatly affected by our life experiences that we enter a period of dryness. At the heart of that dryness is a lack of engagement in dialogue. We do not listen, or if we do we do not respond. We may say we listen but hear nothing. We need to tell the Lord about hearing nothing. Because we believe He knows how we feel we may think there is no reason to tell Him. However, telling Him is not for the Lord's information – it is for the sake of our own openness, our personal engagement in the dialogue.

Known for my capacity to talk the hind leg off a donkey, I find sitting quietly, listening to God, very difficult. But even if I don't hear anything at the time, it will dawn on me later what it was that God was saying. If you have a listening problem, keep at it. God won't stop talking to you and you *will* hear; just be patient.

I hope that something in this chapter will help you to find your way back to faith and to God. If not, there are other ways – keep on exploring until you find the right one for you. We might think we have lost God, left Him somewhere in a happier past, but He is still around. It is a matter of searching, often in surprising places. God is not always where we expect Him to be. He has an uncanny knack of turning up when we least expect Him; perhaps when we would rather He stayed away until we are ready, or have more time, or can find peace and quiet.

*

Wisdom unsearchable
God the invisible,
Love indestructible in frailty appears.
Lord of infinity, stooping so tenderly
Lifts our humanity to the heights of
His throne.

(Extract taken from the song 'Meekness and Majesty' by Graham Kendrick. Copyright © 1986 Thankyou Music)

5

When life in the vicarage goes wrong

Changing times for clergy spouses

It was customary in times past for ordinands to be young unmarried men. Many a romantic novel contained the story of a young woman who married the curate. In the twentieth century two world wars changed things: men returned from the armed forces seeking ordination. They had experience of life (and death). They were accustomed to taking responsibility for their own life and those of others. In addition, in the 1960s and 1970s there was an increase in the number of ordinands in their thirties, forties and fifties, men who had held down responsible posts in business, teaching, the law, etc. Some of them were already married, and theological colleges began accommodating wives and families during ordinands' training.

Unsurprisingly the expectations of today's clergy and their wives are very different from those of the young women marrying young, already ordained, men. They were used to life in a very different world to that of the Church. The confines of life in a parish, the mission field, hospital or other chaplaincy probably seemed narrow and restrictive. But old habits die hard and, even today, clergy spouses and clergy themselves can be expected to conform to an outdated pattern of life. Perhaps dog-collars should come with a spiritual health warning: 'Wearing this may damage your marriage and family relationships.'

Divorce in the vicarage? Unthinkable! Impossible!

For many, contact with a tabloid newspaper is a surreptitious glance at the front page on the way to fetch the daily broadsheet. 'Naughty Vicar' stories so beloved of tabloid journalists do not reach many of the church-going faithful. Those who do read about priests behaving badly, or wives who have run off with a church stalwart, often consider the tales to be over-sensationalized or far-fetched; anyway, it couldn't happen in *our* parish.

So it caused some shock and consternation when, in October 1981, the *Church Times* published an article by Catherine, the divorced wife of an Anglican priest, describing the hell of her marriage breakdown and subsequent divorce. She recounted her difficulties in coping with the loss of her husband, home and income, the intrusion of the media, and how little the church authorities were willing or able to do for her. Catherine was challenging the churches to examine their treatment of people like her. To have the problem placed firmly in the public domain by a serious and respected church newspaper made it uncomfortably real.

Catherine soon received responses from other divorced clergy wives, including one from Philippa, whose husband had told her that he loved another woman, a former parishioner, and wished to marry her. Despite every effort to save the marriage it had reached breaking point and, to cause as little upheaval as possible to their teenage children and the parish, Philippa had left the rectory by mutual agreement, going back to work to keep and house herself. By 1981 she was living in digs and working in London as a secretary.

Philippa and Catherine, who also lived and worked in London, became friends. Realizing they were not alone in their predicament, they set out to locate other clergy wives whose marriages had broken down, to see what could be done for them. Their first target was the practical help they felt should have been forthcoming from the churches, though their spiritual and emotional needs were also important.

At the same time Parliament was considering an amendment to the Clergy Pensions Measure. On the day of the debate John Gummer approached Frank Field (from opposite sides of the House, they shared a Christian faith), asking him to raise a question about the treatment of clergy wives who had been deserted by their husbands. Frank protested that he did not know what John was talking about. No one had mentioned the issue to him. John replied that he had a letter from a clergy wife who had been deserted by her husband; he was asking Frank to raise it in the debate because he was a whip and could not do so himself.

Frank Field did not know then how deep his involvement was to become in the whole question of what happens to clergy wives during and after divorce. Twenty years on he knows only too well, a fact gratefully acknowledged by many ex-wives of clergy.

Frank told Parliament that, while the proposed Measure was welcome, it did nothing for ex-wives of clergymen. His gut reaction, that there was more to this issue, resulted in an appeal for ex-wives to complete a questionnaire, from which he produced a report, *Walking By on the Other Side*. Catherine worked at the House of Commons so was able to respond in person to Frank's report. That, coupled with her link with Philippa, who was by then working for the General Synod, and their shared feeling that more should be done, resulted in Frank's invitation to those who had completed his questionnaire to meet at what was later dubbed by some of those present 'Frank's Tea Party'.

So it was that in January 1983, 28 separated or divorced clergy wives gathered at Frank Field's Westminster office. Mostly unknown to each other, they could not have foreseen that before the teacups had been washed up they would have formed an action and support group to assist clergy wives who, like themselves, had experienced the breakdown of their marriage.

It was not only the rattling of the teacups that January afternoon that echoed in the following months. In the corridors of power of the churches and of Parliament, challenges were faced and hearts and minds were opened to the plight of such women and their children. The causes of these family crises were revealed as many and varied, but for one constant factor: the lack of advice, counselling and support from church authorities. Many wives were reluctant to seek help outside church circles because of the confidential nature of their husband's calling. 'It's a much bigger issue than the Church will admit,' said one. 'It embarrasses them [the church hierarchy] and they want to sweep it under the carpet.' Many bishops when questioned at the time commented, 'Yes, I have heard it does happen, but there have been no cases in my diocese.'

The name Broken Rites was chosen for the group, indicating that the vows made at the rites of ordination and marriage had been broken. As the months passed the forming of link groups created a national network, and the appointment of link members and regional representatives (aptly, for a self-help group, described as Limps and Wrecks by one member of the committee!) enabled members to keep in touch and support each other, either in person or by letter or telephone where distance or finance made meetings difficult, or impossible.

Not long after the formation of Broken Rites, each Church of England bishop appointed at least one Visitor in his diocese, whose task it was to come alongside wives, helping them in their plight, as they struggled to care for their families and rebuild their lives. The non-established churches devised other ways in which to help wives and families, all of which has made life more bearable for divorced wives and their families.

For the members of Broken Rites, old and new, mutual support and friendship is their priority. As churches have increasingly accepted their role in helping with housing and practical matters, the value of friendship and fellowship in the healing of emotional and spiritual wounds is incalculable. Some of the 200 members of Broken Rites have carved out careers for themselves, and several have made new marriages. One (male) visitor to an Annual Meeting expressed his hesitancy in coming – he had expected to find sadness and anger – but commented that he had found hope, laughter and a real sense of resurrection.

Broken Rites publishes a quarterly newsletter, *The Rite Lines*. In addition the group has produced literature giving advice on where and how to obtain help on matters connected with the problems of divorce. Recently the group has found a wider audience through its website. Broken Rites still operates entirely on members' subscriptions and donations from well-wishers. No member is precluded from attending meetings due to lack of finance – travel expenses are readily recoverable. The story of the group's 20-year history is contained in their publication *The Story of Broken Rites – The First Twenty Years* (see 'Helpful addresses', p. 108).

However, we should not lose sight of the fact that sometimes it is the clergyman who is deserted. One deserted clergyman described his sense of being a 'failed priest' as a real issue for clergymen, a feeling shared by several of his ordained friends in a similar situation. The employment set-up of clergy, particularly the 'tied' house, makes marital breakdown among the clergy particularly difficult for them. These are issues which the Church urgently needs to address.

Broken Rites has always been a group for women. It has had enquiries from men but has always suggested they started a group of their own. So far this has not happened, but things may change in the future, especially as more women are being ordained now.

The difficulties and pressures

Although clergy do not 'go out' to work, their working day can vary dramatically in length and the myth that the vicar only works one day a week is a joke. Meanwhile the family may find they are not getting as much interest and attention as they need or, indeed, should have. Clergy wives have been known, in desperation, to book an appointment in their husband's diary because there is no time to discuss even simple family problems. The unspoken feeling that your 'employer' is God, so there can be no contest, elicits feelings of guilt in the spouse, making 'grumbling about the boss' impossible.

Then there is the problem of 'living over the shop'. Today's trend towards a parish office outside the vicarage is a step in the right direction. If arrangements such as church offices, with specific opening hours, can alleviate stress on the vicarage family, they are to be welcomed.

A clergy spouse often feels that their 'other half' belongs to everyone else. Calls for attention, in person or on the telephone, can come at any time, day or night. Mealtimes are often interrupted because 'I knew I would find you at home at dinner time, Vicar'. The spouses of clergy ordained later in life may look back wistfully to the days of the nine-to-five job with free weekends.

One of the biggest sources of stress for families is lack of money. Bringing up a family on a stipend is hard if a clergy spouse is not earning. The cost of children's clothing is frightening, food is a necessity, sometimes heating a large vicarage is kept to an unacceptable minimum in order to economize. Clergy may be provided with housing comparable in size to that of a highly paid executive, without the income to run such a home. Children can feel disadvantaged if their parents can't afford the riding or dancing lessons, play-stations and mobile phones their friends enjoy.

These are only some of the things that can make what should be a happy and fulfilling life a nightmare of worry and strain. Some local congregations are, commendably, making efforts to understand the pressures and offer help where possible.

Expectations of parishioners and of clergy and their spouses

Not so many years ago one wife, new to a home counties parish, was invited to the WI Christmas dinner where wine was served with the meal. A WI member further down the table was heard to comment, 'I see she takes a glass of wine' – whether in appreciation or condemnation, I don't know. Either way, does it matter? The vicar's wife is entitled to behave in a normal fashion, just like other people! She may still today be expected to involve herself in social events, possibly as an organizer, or at least to attend. She may be asked to organize the Sunday School, the flower or the church cleaning rota, or any of a number of practical tasks concerned with the running of the church. There may also be an expectation that she will offer hospitality to church groups at the vicarage, or provide rooms and refreshment for committee meetings. Younger vicars and their more modern wives find these expectations unrealistic as more and more clergy wives have successful careers of their own and limited time to work in parishes. That is not to say that they do not give their husbands wifely support and encouragement, but a parish's expectations put considerable strain on a family that may already be coping with both parents working full time or severe financial difficulties if the wife stays at home.

The increasing number of ordained women in parochial ministry means that the vicarage or curate's house is not going to be manned by a willing volunteer day in and day out, as husbands continue to follow their own careers. It takes a very special kind of man to cope with a wife whose responsibilities mean she may be out at a PCC meeting when he gets home from work, to find his dinner in the oven – if she's had time to cook it!

Clergy and their families have expectations of themselves too. The service of Ordination of Priests requires the priest to promise to strive to fashion his or her own life and that of their household according to the way of Christ. In the same way as promises at marriage are made in good faith and in hope for the future, this promise may become difficult to keep because it depends so much on the behaviour of others. Modern marriage is not a paternal dictatorship; spouses and children may have genuine reasons for unwillingness to behave in particular ways. Some spouses are not Christians or may belong to a different denomination, especially if their husband or wife was a late ordinand and in a secular career at the time of their marriage.

Clergy couples are generally willing to bend to what is perceived to be the will of God. This in turn can cause them to impose expectations on themselves. That the will of the parish may not coincide with the will of God is a matter for discernment and is something each couple needs to work out in prayerful discussion.

Loss of status

There is a certain status to being the vicar's wife. A wife new to a Yorkshire parish learned that 't'vicar's wife is always chairman of Women's Gas'. Never having heard of Women's Gas she wondered if it was a group formed for having a good gossip. But it was a bona fide organization, run under the auspices of the Gas Board, involved in cookery and other gas-related topics. She never discovered how the custom that the vicar's wife should chair the group originated, but continued to do so during the years of her husband's incumbency.

In the days when I was a vicar's wife it did not, apparently, include being vice-chair of the local drama group and appearing in theatrical productions. On the first night of a run of *Blithe Spirit*, in which I played Madame Arcati, as I made my entrance a whisper went round the hall – 'It's Vicar's wife!' Shock horror! Or it may have been pleased amazement! Whatever, it certainly made the audience sit up and take notice!

However, underlying these rather frivolous examples is a serious expectation that you will be a certain kind of person. Even today many people expect the vicar's wife will be a 'lady bountiful' who dispenses 'tea and sympathy' and does 'good works' around the parish. In the eyes of parishioners the incumbent's spouse is very closely allied to the person who is the leader and chief minister of their church, and privy to information they may or may not in fact know. Whether or not this is an accurate assessment, spouses nonetheless occupy a place at the heart of the congregation which is unique.

In the eyes of local people who are not churchgoers there can also be a sense that the vicar's wife or husband is 'different'. At non-church social gatherings I was often asked by a stranger, 'What does your husband do?' The response, 'He's the vicar,' often elicited an intake of breath and a step backwards followed by, 'I'm sorry.' Whether for the poor vicar's wife, or for speaking to her at all, who knows?

The loss of this status after divorce can be hard for a clergy spouse. Having been used to a network of parishioners who were welcoming, helpful, offering to babysit, etc., it is strange to go back to being anonymous, especially in church. Most divorced clergy wives move away from the parish in which their husband served. She may creep in to a new church to sit at the back, just another person in a pew, lonely yet liberated; it is the beginning of the long road back to living.

The public nature of the breakdown

Because clerical clothing is the outward sign of the priestly order, it is impossible for the priest to be anonymous. He or she is seen by the public as an example of holy life, a person of God whose spirituality is not in question, perhaps even one who has answers that elude ordinary mortals. 'Naughty' vicars are newsworthy because they behave like anyone else and we think they shouldn't. It is almost impossible for a clergy divorce to be a private matter. It belongs to the whole church, which needs to be sensitive, caring and non-judgemental to those involved.

Hopefully the response of churches to the problems highlighted by Broken Rites, and greater acceptance generally of divorce, have ensured that people have a better understanding of life in the public eye. Clergy divorce is now more likely to be greeted with sympathy, understanding and offers of help, than with horror and condemnation.

Public attitudes and media attention

Broken Rites uncovered many stories of how the media stripped a wife and family of all vestiges of their dignity. Nowadays the media are more restrained. In the early days there were many tales of the press camping out on vicarage doorsteps. Imagine what that must be like. One can either stay away from home or find some round-about way of getting in and out, unmolested by the press with cameras and microphones. Celebrities are used to this treatment – vicars and their wives and families are not. However, even today a really salacious story of a naughty vicar will grab the headlines in some newspapers. For the family it is a nightmare become real. Marriage breakdown and divorce are painful enough; it hurts to see one's rejection and humiliation blazoned across the front of the *Daily Tabloid*. All the effort put into trying to save the marriage is wiped out in a headline that will be wrapped round tomorrow's fish and chips. Little wonder some Broken Rites' members no longer go to church. Many retain their faith but find corporate worship difficult; some have joined other churches. There is no doubt that marriage breakdown affects us spiritually as well as physically.

Clergy houses

Vicarages are 'tied' houses; once the clergy person leaves the house, the family must follow.

One aspect of this is that the home to which a broken family moves, usually the mother and children, will probably be smaller than the vicarage they have left. This makes life difficult for children, especially perhaps teenagers who have been used to having their own room with space for all the equipment they cannot live without, and room for their friends to sleep over, or just chill out. In the early days of Broken Rites families left alone in the vicarage were given three months' notice to quit, and nowhere to go. At that stage the Church issued notices to quit because they believed, correctly, that it was the only way in which a family could be legally re-housed by the local authority. 'Voluntary homelessness' did not qualify people for re-housing. It took time for Broken Rites to persuade the church authorities that eviction was detrimental to the mental and physical health of deserted wives and families.

Many unfortunate families were offered help only by friends and family. This was an issue of great concern to Broken Rites and one that has been largely solved by churches taking responsibility, with co-operation from church charities and the Church Commissioners, for seeing that wives and families of clergy are not left homeless.

Sexual orientation

'Clergy aren't like *that*.' But under the cassock every priest, male and female, is a human being, with human passions, anger, likes, dislikes and sexual desires.

The debate in the Anglican Church about homosexual priests has relevance for us. It is fairly widely known that there are, and have always been, clergy whose sexual orientation is towards members of their own sex. In times past this has gone unacknowledged. If we don't talk about it we don't have to worry about it. In today's more open social climate these issues have come to the fore. The relevance here is that some clergy marriages fail because the clergyman or woman is homosexual. Writing in *Crucible* Kenneth Jennings, former Dean of Gloucester, says:

It seems to me our church has always sought a safe place – an isolated place – to talk about sexuality, and so failed to be in touch with the wider world of human experience, expanding knowledge, deeper understanding. We kept ourselves very much in the closet and only moved out when pressure was such that we have had to say something, however cautious, even banal. We are seen endlessly to be playing catch-up, rather than contributing thoughtfully to the ongoing exploration of all that is involved in human life and relationships.

Biologically we now know that every fertilised egg in the human womb has the capacity initially to develop into a male or female foetus. The vast majority develop in such a way that there is no doubt about their eventual gender . . . in most cases the phenomenon of homosexuality is, in the words of Michael Mayne, 'the result of a natural orientation, something given'. He goes on to say: 'That is no longer in question.' The Church in general is still very reluctant to acknowledge and live with that conclusion.

Christine McMullen, Chairman of Broken Rites, writing in the same edition of *Crucible* about clergy marriage, says:

I met a respected clergyman who was about to retire. I asked where he was retiring to and he named a far distant city. Surprised at the choice, I asked why and he said that his wife had died recently and this released him in retirement to follow the gay lifestyle he knew to be his orientation; he felt a city offered more possibility of finding a like-minded companion. He said that his grown-up children were surprised but supportive.

At about the same time a fairly young clergyman with two teenage children told me that he was gay and that, when his wife found another partner to marry, they would divorce and he would come out. In time this happened. She got married and the children stayed with him and they saw their mother regularly. This seemed a very careful and planned response to the difficulty. He said they had both been brought up in strict Evangelical households and had no sexual experience before marriage – so he had no idea that he preferred same-sex partners.

The two cases are representative of the wide range of problems which homosexuality in a clergyman can cause his family and parish. Many of the difficulties are quite different from those experienced by heterosexual families, and need different approaches and treatment.

Fortunately Broken Rites can offer help to women in many different situations. The group has a confidential list of people prepared to befriend someone having a similar experience to her own. The countrywide network of support groups is important. Christine McMullen tells of one local group recently taken aback by an angry and volatile woman wanting to know what the Church is thinking about, letting her ex-husband stay in ministry when he is known to have male partners, while she is despatched from the vicarage as if she never existed.

These illustrations show how important a topic this is in the area of marriage and marriage breakdown. The churches have dragged their heels over such matters, by not facing up to the problems or actively encouraging openness. Many homosexual men have married to satisfy the requirement of parishes for a married priest with a family. Christine McMullen concludes:

> What is needed is to avoid unnecessary guilt and shame being felt by the family members. Society today is far less judgmental of people who adopt a gay lifestyle, and is more prepared to discuss openly issues arising from bisexual/gay people who regret an earlier heterosexual marriage. This does not mean that promiscuity should be endorsed, but by failing to be transparent and open . . . the Church heaps guilt and shame on a couple who already have problems enough.

This is not only a problem in clergy marriages. Homosexual and lesbian people may marry heterosexual partners for differing reasons. Just how difficult it must be to live that sort of lie most of us cannot begin to imagine, nor the hell into which their spouse may descend when they learn about their partner's sexual orientation. Partners in these situations need to find a way to re-establish not only their daily life, but also their spiritual life.

*

Because clergy and their families are human it is no wonder that sometimes life in the vicarage goes wrong. In some instances a spouse who is unhappy and dissatisfied with their way of life may look elsewhere for what they feel is missing.

Frances' story is not untypical. After joining Broken Rites she gave an interview which attracted much attention and brought many offers of support, as well as potential members. When her husband left her and her three children after admitting to a series of affairs, she had no idea where to turn for help and felt completely isolated. She thought no one in the church hierarchy would believe her story, since her husband was a clergyman and supposed to be above 'that sort of thing'. She reckoned that everyone in the parish would be equally incredulous. She felt totally alone and ignored.

In the early days of Broken Rites many clergy wives felt the same. The Church had ceased to be a support for them. Some of them found that they could no longer continue to be part of a worshipping community; others felt they had lost their faith altogether. But they have found mutual support, friendship, help and comfort in their membership of Broken Rites, as they journey to a new life.

*

Beginning at the End

I lived with love
And thought that was enough
To fill a world with joy and laughter,
But it brought tears and pain, after
Many love-torn years.

I lived with hope
That love would still hold fast
Our longings, dreams and sweet desires;
But through mistrust and unbelief, the fires
Of hope burned brief.

I lived with faith
Which should have been the first, not last;
Love, Hope and Faith brought pain
Faith, Hope and Love will bring back joy again.

© Pauline Druiff, 1982

6

Who am I?

*We are all in the gutter, but some of us
are looking at the stars.*
(Oscar Wilde)

And those stars are reachable, even from the gutter. There we will find our whole self again. Before we can make that journey we need to take a close look at ourselves. I once read that facing up to unpleasant facts about yourself and your situation can lead to a new maturity. After my divorce I certainly learned some things about myself that I did not like. Conversely I discovered talents of which I was previously unaware and a strength of character which had lain dormant for most of my life.

Writing has always been a way in which I have worked through my problems and emotions. Sometimes it is poetry, sometimes prose, or maybe just a letter, which I probably won't send. Putting things on paper has a way of clearing the mind and helping to get things in perspective. Some time ago I wrote an article entitled 'One Woman's Place', as a basis for a talk. I guess I was at that point when I was still searching for where that place might be.

It occurred to me that who we are is closely allied to where we are and what we are at any given time in our life. In order to think more clearly about this I jotted down all the people I had been in my life who were connected to either where I was or what I was doing. It turned out to be a long list! I started as a baby and moved on to be a toddler, a schoolgirl, daughter, student, girl friend, shorthand typist/secretary, fiancée, bride, wife/clergy-wife (same only different!), mother, divorcee, housemistress, personal secretary, fiancée and bride (again) and pensioner. You can probably make a similar list for yourself. What is so mind-boggling is that one person can be so many things during a lifetime. Apart from those descriptions I am also a writer, a painter, a 'rag-rugger', member and past chairman of Broken Rites, ex-PCC secretary, and many more which are connected with my church membership, hobbies and interests. These versions of the adult 'me' may be connected with how I see myself, and how I project my image to others; how I *want* them to see me.

Think of a circus clown and we see a white face painted with enormous eyes and enlarged lips, a 'bald' wig fringed with ginger fuzz, baggy clothes and funny shoes. But who is underneath all that? Who is this clown? He may be a very serious and academic person, perhaps even a depressive character; but we see someone funny, jolly and entertaining. The clown wants to project a very definite image which is not necessarily a reflection of his real self.

Most of us do what the clown does – often unknowingly, sometimes deliberately. We want people to see us in a particular way, one that perhaps doesn't come naturally to us. We give an impression to others without always realizing what that impression is.

When Bob met me his first impression was, 'This lady is very prim and proper. I'd better mind my p's and q's.' Fortunately it didn't take long for me to demolish that impression by just being myself! How sad that we are prepared to reveal to others only as much of ourselves as we think they need. And who are we to judge? What we decide we should be like may not be God's idea of who, or where, He wants us to be.

'One Woman's Place' was an attempt to define my own place in the scheme of things and to show that the old saying 'A woman's place is in the home' is only partly true. Yes, I am still a housewife in spite of all the other parts of my life; I still shop, wash, cook, clean and do all those jobs which a woman is still,

even in today's world, often expected to do. But our own aspirations, the way we project our image, and how we behave, all
need bearing in mind especially when we think about moving
on (see Chapter 7).

*

Although divorce is devastating at the time it is possible to look
back afterwards and see that good has come out of it. One man
who felt his life was in ruins realized that God was calling him
to move on, to grow up. 'You don't teach a child to walk always
holding his hand,' he said. 'You have to step back sometimes
and allow it to totter towards you. It's as if God sometimes
takes a few steps back and makes us reach out more.' It may
often feel as if you are taking a step forward and sliding two
steps back, but eventually you realize you are slowly becoming
a whole person again. The face you see in the bathroom mirror
is only the outside. Inside is a complicated human being, a hurting human being, but a human being capable of surviving. To
do that you need to go on a journey of discovery – to find yourself. And that will be easier with God alongside than doing it on
your own.

The place where we live our inner life during marriage breakdown and divorce has been described in many different ways. I
found myself in a deep pit with such steep sides it appeared to
be impossible to climb out. A friend spoke of being in a bare
room with no doors or windows. Another friend was in a dark
tunnel with no apparent light at the end of it. Wherever you are,
or were, in yours, I expect it will be somewhere similar. An
unfriendly place with no visible means of escape.

It is on arrival in this place that we finally lose our sense of
who we are. In our own eyes we have become a nobody, a
worthless individual with no self-belief or confidence in our
abilities. This is where we begin our journey to the stars.

Self-esteem

Low, or non-existent, self-esteem is common among separated and divorced people. There are many things which help in combatting this, and for Christians the most obvious one is prayer. We believe that God loves us, no matter what. We can be the biggest failure in the world, the fattest or thinnest, plainest or most beautiful, it makes no difference to Him. We are valued for ourselves – not what we do, or how we look, but who we *are*. It is likely that at such a low point in our lives we have lost the ability to accept this, even to pray. It is hard to believe He still cares about us – since He has in our eyes allowed this terrible thing to happen. We are not valued by anyone, even Him. Not true! Not true! Some of us who have 'been there, done that' would like to print a T-shirt saying 'HE *DOES* VALUE YOU!'

What can be done to recover our self-esteem? We all need to find our own way, but for me it was working. This was a real necessity anyway – I had nowhere to live and no income. To go back to work in late middle age is not the easiest thing in the world and I took a job as a housemistress in a girls' boarding school – for which I had no training apart from bringing up a family. This kept me totally occupied for long hours during term time, and gave me time in the holidays to spend with my own children. It was demanding and absorbing being 'mother' to 70 adolescent girls, but extremely good for my self-esteem. I was 'looked up to', consulted about all manner of problems, treated as an authority. I was given respect, as well as affection and loyalty. What a gift to someone who thought she was nothing. After three years I was ready to get back to what I was trained to do and started by temping as a secretary before finally finding a post as a personal secretary where I stayed until I retired.

It is impossible for me to tell every reader what is the best path for them, but think about your life, your skills, your training, even your inclinations, and use all those to find the way back to self-esteem in the community.

Confidence

Self-confidence is closely linked to self-esteem. Remember those days when we had all the confidence in the world? There was nothing we could not do if we tried. Admittedly there were times when over-confidence caused us to fall flat on our face, but the confidence of youth is such that we were able to pick ourselves up and move on to the next thing. The end of a marriage, especially one that has lasted a long time, will knock away all our props. Our confidence will suffer and we will be unable to believe that we can do anything worthwhile. It is important not to lose heart: we need to listen to what others are saying or we may miss comments which will boost our confidence and help on the path to finding enough of it to take on a new or difficult task – even building a new life for ourselves.

When I was first looking for a way of existing after the end of my marriage, I had a strong urge to take a course and become a social worker. I even found a place at a university where I could do this. All I needed then was a place to live – digs would do – and the confidence to actually take the plunge. But confidence was something I had little of at that time. Instead, as I have said, I went to work in a school where my skills as a parent and homemaker could be put to use. I just did not have enough confidence in myself to contemplate anything else.

It is a sad state of affairs when marriage strips a person of confidence in their own abilities. It can result from some of the things described in Chapter 1, verbal and physical abuse in particular, but it can simply be lack of affirmation from one's spouse. Compliments for, say, arranging the flowers or cooking a nice meal may not in themselves be very important, but they are a vital and welcome affirmation of our skills, of ourselves, and an acknowledgement that we are valued.

Rebuilding self-confidence is not quick – remember, it took me three years before I had enough confidence to go back to secretarial work. Many times I have found myself telling people 'be gentle with yourself'. We need to have patience and allow ourselves to slip back those two steps sometimes.

Learning to live alone

Lonely

Lonely lonely for a hand to hold
For a strong arm around me again
For someone to talk to and share with and love
For someone to love me To need and value me
Lonely for touching For eating For sleeping together
Lonely in the park At a party With families
On holiday When I wake up On a long journey
Decision times In a beautiful sunset Watching TV
Oh God I'm lonely. God. Silence.
Amidst all the noise there's a silence around me
A silence inside me
There's still unreality and disbelief
Sometimes it's worse than others Like now
A drifting a floundering in space It's spatial
It's disconnected from solid
In my head floating unattached unreal
And time is all jumbled up Then. Now. Before Then.
Who am I? Who was I? What am I like?
What will happen to me?
There are moments when words can't describe it
Sort of spinning dizzy non-coherent moments
Without thoughts
With just frightening feelings. They pass
And I'm back with the questions. And reality.

© Sarah Thorley, 1990
(reproduced with permission)

Sarah adds:

I came across this recently, shoved away in a drawer, written about 18 months after our 17 years of marriage had ended. Reading it evoked the feelings again and reminded me of how compelling I have found it, at the worst times, to write; it is almost as if the physical act of spilling out the words on to paper removes a measure of the pain inside me and lightens the load. Perhaps others find the same.

There are other more positive emotions expressed in some of Sarah's poems written as she progressed along her journey of recovery.

*

As I write I want to say of each section – this is the hardest one to do. They can't all be the hardest, so perhaps I should say that each stage of this journey is equally hard. Living alone is not easy when you have been used to a noisy, busy, family life. I successfully avoided having to live entirely alone for some time; after the time in school I spent several months in digs before I finally got a flat of my own. It was a terrific feeling to have a home of my own again, to be able to furnish it, albeit sparsely, as I wanted, to paint the walls the colours I liked. The quietness was deafening. I was used to teenagers playing loud music – a different pop song in every room, battling with the constantly switched-on TV – so I rattled around alone rather like a dried pea in a large pod. The flat was in central London and, moving from the country, I was nervous about mugging and other things which I knew could happen to a person in an inner city. For the first three months I would go to work in the morning, come home in the evening and then stay put until work again the next day. I was scared to go out. Eventually I realized that my fears were keeping me a prisoner in my own home and I found the courage to start going out in the evening – mostly to a film or concert on my own, sometimes with new friends made at work or through Broken Rites. I had the company of my goddaughter for several weeks, which helped on my way to total independence. Later on, after I had become used to my own company, my son and my daughter both moved to London and came to share the flat with me.

Living alone does not have to be lonely. I was fortunate, I had not lost my faith nor left the Church, so I quickly became integrated into my local parish church and found friendship and fellowship there. A full-time job takes up a lot of time, but then the holidays come round. I imagine most readers will have become used, as I had, to family holidays. Having a holiday alone for the first time is daunting. At the beginning I stayed with friends or relatives, which was a familiar activity from the past and therefore unthreatening. After a while it seemed sensible to try going away on my own. Bravely I hired a car for a week and set off touring round Sussex and Kent, staying in B&Bs. It was a wonderfully freeing experience. One advantage of the single life is being able to please oneself; where one goes, what time one eats and sleeps, how long one stays just looking at a view. The down side is having no one to talk to about it and share it all with. But that first holiday taught me that not only could I live alone, I could travel alone too.

Looking after yourself

Perhaps not quite as hard as some of the things we learn on our journey of discovery, but often more difficult than we expect. Being a busy spouse and parent is largely about looking after other people, one's partner and children. As we grow older many of us have an aged or ailing parent to care for too. It is easy to get used to putting oneself at the back of the queue – mothers in particular will recognize the habit of giving others the 'best' bit of the joint, the crispiest roast potatoes, even going without something if there is not quite enough to go round. So looking after ourselves is something we have perhaps not done since bachelor days.

My birthday came around a few months after I began living alone. I was still at the stage of not going out in the evening and my children were living at opposite ends of the country, so I prepared myself to celebrate alone. I came home from work with fillet steak, mushrooms, tomatoes, pâté, a bottle of red wine and a Marks & Spencer trifle. This was to be my birthday celebration meal. I duly cooked and ate it in solitary state, and had drunk two-thirds of the wine when the phone rang. A young friend wanted to say 'Happy Birthday'; I responded slightly tipsily. A few minutes later came another call – my daughter; then my son rang; then a very old friend; then another one. Although I rather wished I had not looked after myself quite so well, and gone more slowly with the wine, it turned out to be a very happy occasion – so many people were thinking of me. I was not alone after all.

In many ways learning to live alone is a luxury. There *is* no one else to please. We have all the time in the world to concentrate on our own well being. Just as well if we are still recovering from a shattered life. Nonetheless, the temptation to become overly selfish is to be resisted. An elderly lady, a widow, once said to me how very lonely it was living alone. Another widow who lived on her own, overhearing her remark, commented, 'I never feel alone – I know that I am not alone. The Lord is always with me.' That seemed to me to be a wonderful way to live, sure in the knowledge of the Lord's presence. Even though I was still a churchgoer, I did not always feel, as that lady did, that God was with me. It took a lot longer for that to become a reality for me again.

Friendships

> *Don't walk in front of me, I may not follow.*
> *Don't walk behind me, I may not lead.*
> *Walk beside me, and be my friend.*
> (Albert Camus)

Gina, who described her faith as having been 'shot out of the water' by her divorce says:

My faith is linked to my circle of friends. I was fortunate. I was able to keep lots of them. Over and above anything else, they are responsible for my continuing walk with God. I would recommend cherishing Christian friends, even when they said stuff I didn't want to hear.

I have come to realize that wise friends are a priceless commodity. Friends who were not afraid to point out truths to me. Friends who were not afraid to tell me that 'your friends can't do this any more, we are getting upset, you need to go and talk to someone else outside the situation, you need to do it soon.'

I certainly say 'amen' to that. What a wonderful description of the value of friends when we are in trouble. Perhaps even more than relatives, friends can support us in spiritual as well as practical ways. They are able to see us without the rose-coloured glasses that our parents or other family members may wear. Friends know us as we are – there are no preconceived notions in their minds about how or who we ought to be. We are we; just that. And the best friends are those who can tell us the truth, in love.

During my low time I had two friends in particular who gave me so much that I once said to one of them, 'I can never repay you for all you have done for me.' Chris replied: 'You don't have to. Just pass it on.' What wise words. I have tried to live up to my promise to do what she asked. Not always successfully, but hopefully God forgives the lapses.

Both these friends were generous not only with their time but with practical help, sharing their homes and families with me. Joan and her husband invited me to join their family Christmas on a number of occasions so that my family and theirs are now inextricably entwined. The memories of those times are precious. Chris gave me a key to her front door when I first went to work in the school. 'You never need to say you have nowhere to go,' she said, as she handed me the sheets to make up 'my' bed in 'my' room. My days off and parts of the school holidays were spent as part of her family. For everything these two did for me there are not enough thanks. Later I told Joan that I was a changed person. She replied I had simply gone back to being the person I had been before. I had finally found myself again –

and, what joy, I was still the person who had become her friend 40 years before.

Job's comforters

Having praised the value of such true friendship as both Gina and I have experienced, I should also issue a note of caution. It has been said that it is in adversity that you discover who your friends are. This, like many of the old sayings, is very true. Our best and truest friends are those who act as Gina's did for her and Chris and Joan did for me. There are others who consider themselves friends, and who you include among your friends, but they may actually be a hindrance rather than a help. These kindly and well-meaning people offer platitudes and 'there, there' sympathy. They find nothing positive to say or do to help. In biblical terms they are 'Job's comforters':

> When Job's three friends, Eliphaz the Temanite, Bildad the Shuhite and Zophar the Naamathite, heard about all the troubles that had come upon him, they set out from their homes and met together by agreement to go and sympathise with him and comfort him. When they saw him from a distance, they could hardly recognise him; they began to weep aloud, and they tore their robes and sprinkled dust on their heads. Then they sat on the ground with him for seven days and seven nights. No one said a word to him, because they saw how great his suffering was.
>
> (Job 2.11–13, NIV)

A shoulder to cry on is a very necessary thing when one is in trouble, but weeping with you and simply wiping away your tears is not enough. Job's friends were rendered speechless by his plight; friends like that can perpetuate the misery instead of alleviating it. Although sympathy is meant kindly, sometimes kindness can kill; it can encourage us to wallow in our own misery, instead of fighting to be free of it. If some of your friends are of the 'never mind' or 'he/she's not worth it' brigade, it may be better to avoid them until you feel stronger. The blunt truth handed out by a true friend is worth all the hankies and shoulders. It can be quite comforting sometimes to feel sorry for oneself, but it is so obstructive to recovery and renewal that it is not worth the time spent on it.

*

A friend has lent me a book of religious exercises and devotions dated 1625. The book is written in Old English with s's printed as f's, but amazingly some of the devotions speak just as strongly to us today as they did to people more than 400 years ago. Here is a selection; some of them could have been written for me. How about you?

- Almighty and most wise Creator who has made me of nothing, suffer me not to make myself worse than nothing.
- When thou made me light, I made myself darkness, but thou hast turned my darkness into light.
- When I was freed, I enthralled myself, but thou hast freed me.
- When I was straight, I crooked my will, but thou hast rectified me.
- When I was whole I maimed myself, but thou hast healed me.
- When I was happy I made myself miserable, but thou hast restored me to my former bliss.

*

Memories

Memories are both
Joy and sorrow entwined
As the honeysuckle entwines the briar
Grief is the loss of that which gave joy
Shall both be cast away
Because the briar is too painful?
Or shall I rather unravel the honeysuckle
Feel the pain of the thorns
Take the time, find the way
To let go of the briar
To hold and drink deeply
The scent of the honeysuckle
For it is healing to look and to smell
And thus can the memories be treasured.

And yet spurn not the briar
For it was a means of growth
A way to light, to life
To who I am.

© Sarah Thorley, 1996
(reproduced with permission)

7

Moving on

I know without a doubt that this separation was the best thing for our whole family. I would not, I think, do it any differently. I stayed in a horrid situation for over 15 years. Why? I wanted to be an active parent and I had no career, having stopped teaching, by choice, on marriage.

(A member of Broken Rites in *The Rite Lines*)

Moving on is the last thing we can think of when we first enter the limbo-land of marriage breakdown. We cling to the past, constantly looking back. A cautionary tale: my friend's adult son walked into town to do some shopping. He came back with a lump on the back of his head. When asked what had caused it he replied, 'I walked into a lamp post.' His mother, puzzled, asked how he hit the back of his head doing that. 'I was looking backwards,' he said. A silly story, but it taught me that looking where you are going is always a better plan than gazing at where you have been!

Divorce itself does not necessarily jog us into starting our journey to recovery. Anyway, you may ask, where do you go when you are in the bottom of a pit or the darkness of a tunnel? But slowly, very slowly, the top of the pit and the light at the end of the tunnel become visible. My experience of being in a black pit is that you have to find a way out, perhaps metaphorically scrambling up the walls, hanging on by your fingernails as I did. Painfully and slowly I eventually reached the top, where my journey began in earnest. I saw the ground ahead sloping gently upwards towards distant mountains and knew I had to walk across the plain and climb up. By the time I reached the foothills I was stronger and more positive – climbing the mountain had become a real possibility. I was on the way!

Of course, happy endings don't come without some pain and hardship, some successes and other awful flops; some good decisions and other horrible, best-forgotten mistakes. I experienced all of those, and more, but hope that even the worst things have contributed to making me the person I now am – who, as my friend Joan commented, is not too different from the person I was before all this happened. We come full circle and meet ourselves, healed and whole, again.

For those whose children are grown up there is the possibility they may have to go back to work, either full time or part time. Then there is the opportunity to make new relationships with people of both sexes. If we have moved away from where we lived as a married person, it may be necessary for our survival to make new friendships and find companionship where we are now living. And finally we need to consider the next stage of our life bearing in mind our age and family circumstances.

The world of work

For many men and women who are already employed, perhaps following a demanding career, the world of work is not strange or daunting. Others – probably fewer and fewer as time passes – will be faced with returning to work after a lengthy period of homemaking and child-rearing. If you are one of the latter, the first thing to do is to consider what you have actually been trained for and what other skills you have acquired during your life. It may be that you do not want to go back to the sort of work you did before, possibly in the early days of your marriage. Teaching, for instance, could be difficult to return to because of changes in methods and the way in which schools are organized. But that training may still have its uses; perhaps teaching English as a Foreign Language might be up your street, or working in a kindergarten where training in infant teaching may still be relevant. If you were trained to teach secondary school age children, there may be a use for your skills in examination marking – perhaps preceded by a little revision of your own – or private tutoring. There are many ways in which our early training can be used.

My own skills of shorthand and typing have always been in demand but the keyboard I am using today is a far cry from the old Underwood typewriter I learned on umpteen years ago! When I finally went back to secretarial work I was amazed at the technology of an electric typewriter with a carriage which went shooting back at the touch of a key, now old-fashioned compared with today's advanced technology. But here I am with a computer at home, surfing the net, sending emails and doing all manner of things which were unheard of a couple of decades ago.

If the need to work arises before you have fully recovered your equilibrium, not to mention confidence, try something simple and untaxing. A gentle way back into the employment market will boost confidence and give you breathing space to retrain or brush up your existing skills. No one is without value. We all have marketable skills. Many successful entrepreneurs started with a 'cottage industry', baking cakes or making jam in their own homes. Talk to your friends – you may find you have skills you didn't know about, or that have remained rusty for so long you had forgotten them.

It is important not to try and run before you can walk, so study the job ads in the papers, the cards in the newsagents' windows. It is amazing how many people nowadays earn money by doing housework for others who don't have the energy (or the inclination) any more. Though not mentally taxing, it needs a certain amount of physical strength and a friendly and reliable nature. Ironing is another chore which many people welcome help with and, if you are one of those people who actually likes it (are there any?), is a useful service to provide. There is a great demand for gardeners, of either sex, and decorators too. If your homemaking skills have included painting and decorating or cultivating the garden, there are many elderly people who would welcome getting 'a lady' in as opposed to a man. If you can fit your skills and personality to a job, you can really enjoy being back in the world of work again.

New relationships – male and female

Making new relationships with members of one's own sex need not be a problem, but will depend a lot on where one works. In an office, a shop or some place where there are quite a number of employees, it is not too difficult to become friendly with others. Or joining a club might be an option. If you are still attending church the after-service tea/coffee provides a good opportunity to make new acquaintances. Of course, people won't rush up to you wanting to be an instant friend; it takes effort on your part too, but as time passes you will find you have made a circle of new friends.

One 'survivor' writes:

So how does one survive? I found the only thing I could do was to stand still, step outside myself as it were and try to look at my life and problems as if they belonged to someone else. Not a very easy thing to do but finding that I did not have any confidence or strength to trust anyone else – particularly anyone involved with the church – I decided that I could only trust myself. I would not let myself down and so 'treating myself as someone else' became the order of the day. I would assess a difficulty on the lines of 'How would I tell someone else to deal with that?' I then gave myself the answer and literally forced myself to do it. I went to an accommodation agency because I ordered myself to do it and rented a couple of rooms in a bungalow in a totally unknown area. I needed to get to know a few people. I went to the local library to find out what sort of club activities there were locally and made myself go to the nearby folk club, smiling as I went through the door and saying 'hello' to people. After making myself do this for a few weeks, I found I was accepted and at least had some folks to say 'hello' to if I passed them in the street.

(A Broken Rites member in *The Rite Lines*)

Making a new life will not be easy but, as this brave lady's grit and determination show, it can be done.

The delicate subject of making new relationships with members of the opposite sex is one that is often not spoken of in public. It was some time after the start of Broken Rites before my local group decided to 'theme' one of our Sunday lunch meetings and discuss 'Making New Relationships', in particular with men. I had already joined a singles group in London, mostly because it is difficult for a woman on her own to have much of a social life in the city. There was also a company that advertised weekend breaks for singles and I had enjoyed two of those. A widowed friend suggested answering adverts in a singles magazine, but the stories about some of those contacts are rather hair-raising (more suitable for a work of fiction – proving that truth certainly is stranger!). Our group meeting revealed that I was not the only member of Broken Rites looking for ways of making new relationships. We learned of one member's experience of a meeting after answering an ad. Having arranged to meet a gentleman for the first time, she had agreed (most unwisely) that he would pick her up at a certain place at a certain time in his Mini. She arrived at the rendezvous a little early and waited. At the appointed time a gentleman drove up in a Mini and stopped. She opened the door and jumped in. Surprised and rather put out the driver said, 'Excuse me, you're sitting on my sandwiches!' Needless to say it was the wrong Mini and the wrong man. We all laughed so much we forgot to ask if the right one ever turned up – or if she even waited!

However, for me the singles group was a good way of meeting people, of both sexes. When asked later I commented that I met a lot of very congenial women, attractive, intelligent and with bags of personality, but that most of the men were 50+ (and some) hoping to meet either a young blonde bombshell for 'fun', or an older woman who was good for cooking meals and darning socks. Since I didn't fit into either of those categories (well, I did the older bit – I just wasn't into the cooking and darning part!) I just enjoyed the sociability of the group and made good friends, both male and female.

However, introduction agencies may be more successful, as one divorcee writes:

> Six years after my marriage ended I joined an introduction agency. This won't be the way for everyone, but it's been good for me. I didn't even want to think about a new relationship for several years after the painful break-up of my marriage (but I was lonely). Then within the space of a month three different friends suggested it and encouraged me with stories of others for whom it had worked. 'No, no, no!' I protested, 'I can't imagine anyone I would want to meet doing such a thing!'
>
> About three months later a widowed friend came to stay and we bought the Saturday *Times*. Out of curiosity and with many giggles, we combed the 'Saturday Rendezvous' page. Egging each other on we phoned up a few of the agencies and asked for brochures. It became more intriguing. I still felt embarrassed by the whole idea and even rather ashamed that it had 'come to this', but a sense of humour and of adventure prevailed and the upshot was that I did join one of the agencies. I've had no bad experiences, although there were some months when nothing happened and that made me feel a 'failure'.
>
> Although I've met about twenty men and had some very interesting conversations and some fun evenings – several drinks, a dozen meals out, a couple of concerts, a couple of country walks – I've never felt unsafe . . . they were all pleasant and interesting people and some sad stories were shared. And that might have been that, but the very last person I met before my membership ran out has become someone very special to me. I don't know how it will end up but whatever happens in the future I'm really glad to have met him; it has been a healing experience for both of us and we have the agency system to thank!
>
> (A Broken Rites member in *The Rite Lines*)

Both these experiences need to be viewed with caution. In a singles group or when answering an advert we are very dependent on believing what people tell us about themselves. We may be honest and open, but not everyone is like that. There is risk in any relationship, but meeting strangers can be dangerous if we are not aware of how to spot a situation becoming hard to handle, or some behaviour in a person that might lead to difficulties. Those of us who have had long marriages have become unused to the world of meeting, flirting, socializing with strangers and going to bars and restaurants without a partner. The first time I attempted to join the singles club I was afraid to enter the pub where they met. I must have looked pretty suspicious hanging around outside, especially as it was close by Charing Cross Station! I eventually chickened out and went home, but was back the next week with more courage. If we are not ready for this sort of adventure it is better to wait until we are. Unused to entering public places of entertainment alone, we feel conspicuous and awkward. Hardly the best frame of mind in which to 'make friends and influence people'.

On the occasions when I arranged to meet gentlemen I did not know I was always careful to make sure it was in a public place, where there were likely to be lots of people around. Hotel lounges, coffee bars, railway stations, and so on, are usually safe. Never, never invite anyone to your home until you have got to know them well; and never accept an invitation to theirs.

The next stage of life

We may expect to slide effortlessly from one stage of our lives to the next. However, after divorce it may not be so easy. Each of us will have different 'next stages'. One friend of mine went back to university in middle age. It must have been difficult being a mature student among all those young people. But she coped, got her degree, spent a year in the USA and the dreams of her youth were fulfilled. It was that experience which probably gave her the confidence to move gracefully and contentedly into retirement and grandmother-hood.

Most married couples have dreams: of what they will achieve, the type of house they will live in and, if they are over 45, where they will retire. My husband and I always had a dream of a house in the country with a stream running through the garden, surrounded by fields and woods. Failing that, a bungalow by the sea and a dog to walk with along the sands. The reality for me, before I met Bob, my second husband, was a rented flat in Pimlico and a pretty meagre pension. However, I was fortunate and at least I have accomplished the 'by the sea' bit, although not a bungalow and only muddy sand at low tide. No dog, either. But then happiness is not dependent on what you have and where you live. As I say, moving on, without so much as blinking, to the next stage of life may not be easy after divorce, but once you have done it you will have a great sense of achievement. I have mentioned elsewhere that being single means not having to consult or consider anyone else. Of course, we may still have children or other people for whom we are responsible, but generally speaking it will be possible for us to make our own choice about the next stage of our life. You may not be financially able to have a lot of choice in where you live, but how you live will be up to you. I admire the 'survivor' quoted earlier in the chapter who moved to a completely new area. She continued:

As the months went by I was becoming stronger and more able to face my new situation. I had a roof over my head and a job of work, which paid my rent and other expenses. I was now a person in my own right. I could make my own decisions and did not have to fit in with someone else.

Yes, there is life after divorce. Do not expect it to gel overnight – it will be a painful struggle but you will survive. Your own personality will surface and your confidence in yourself will return. Try my trick of stepping outside yourself so that you can see your problems as if they were someone else's. Give yourself that helpful guidance and advice you would offer others. For you will find your advice will work better for you than anyone else's.

(A member of Broken Rites in *The Rite Lines*)

*

I hope that these illustrations will fire you with the confidence to take your life in your hands and move on. A broken marriage can never be forgotten, but it can be put behind us and left in the past, where it belongs. The person we become as we grow in maturity is the sum total of all our experiences. Those experiences can influence us either for good or for ill. The choice is ours, so be bold: don't allow your experiences of the knocks in life to push you down, but rise above them, look to the future and create a new life for yourself. This is something you need to do for yourself. But there is always help at hand; you only have to ask and God will be there with you. He knows 'you're worth it'.

*

Make time for stillness and quiet
to listen to the Spirit –
who makes all things new.

8

Marrying again

The Puzzle

What have you done to me?
Why do I feel this way?
The tender feelings you evoke
Grow stronger every day.
You are not tall and handsome
Nor yet a millionaire,
There seems to be no reason why
I should walk on air.

I've tried to analyse
The way I feel for you;
At each attempt to do so
The mistier is the view.
Perhaps I'll just accept it,
Not try to understand
The warmth when we're together
Walking hand in hand.

I know that you are gentle,
Kind and loving, too,
You want to make things right for me
As I do too – for you.
We may need to do nothing
But wait a while and see
What lies ahead along the road
Of life for you and me.
© Pauline Druiff, 1987

A success story

I wrote this poem in my mid-fifties when a blossoming relation-ship with a 65-year-old widower seemed to be 'getting serious'. I was very happy and, by then, well past the stage of being unable to even contemplate a new marriage. I had spent nine years alone and met Bob quite by chance on a winter break in the Mediterranean. He had been widowed for almost 20 years; we shared a wacky sense of humour; parts of our childhood and young lives had been spent in the same areas. We had a lot in common and as time progressed we both wanted to put our relationship on a legally committed basis and get married.

As a Christian I had some misgivings about the marriage, mainly because Bob is not a Christian – he was born and brought up in a Jewish family. However, through prayer and sharing my concerns with those close to me, I came to believe that this marriage was right for us. That God was blessing me with a second chance. I could not, however, feel it would be right to marry in church. First, I felt I simply could not, in all conscience, make the same promises I had already made 35 years previously to another person, even though I felt I had God's blessing. Second, because Bob was not a Christian it seemed inappropriate to ask him to marry in a Christian church. The Register Office in Richmond, Surrey, was fine, and I am sure God is very used to attending civil weddings.

We both believe that we have made a commitment for life and are serious about that. My second marriage has been – as described by a clergyman friend when I told him of my engage-ment – 'the triumph of hope over experience'! That we made the right decision is borne out by the fact that we are still very happy together, caring for each other as we move further into the later stages of life, still laughing at the same things, still talking about every subject under the sun – able to communicate in an open and honest way.

Is it OK to marry again?

On the matter of remarriage after divorce, Glad Bryce wrote:

> Some of the biblical references to divorce specify the right to remarriage. The divorce standards set down in the Old Testament included the conditions for remarriage.
>
>> Suppose a man marries a woman and later decides that he doesn't want her, because he finds something about her that he doesn't like. So he writes out divorce papers, gives them to her, and sends her away from his home. Then suppose she marries another man, and he also decides that he doesn't want her, so he also writes out divorce papers, gives them to her and sends her away from his home. Or suppose her second husband dies. In either case, her first husband is not to marry her again; he is to consider her defiled. If he married her again, it would be offensive to the LORD.
>>
>> (Deuteronomy 24.1–4, Good News Bible)
>
> Remarriage was part of the reason for making divorce possible. Divorce allowed the marriage to be dissolved so that remarriage could take place. Divorce in the Old Testament was a way of making relationships legal.
>
> When Jesus spoke about these standards, he was attempting to point out how destructive some of them were. Women were especially hurt by the society of his time. In Matthew chapter 5 he spoke of the ineffectiveness of the divorce standards: 'When one divorces his wife . . . he makes her commit adultery.' Jesus wanted to teach how unjust it was for a man to remarry with no repercussions; [while] the woman was doomed to adultery because of the divorce. Some Christians interpret his words literally and believe that the person who remarries while the former spouse is still living is committing adultery.
>
> When I first conducted the course for the Anglican Church in Toronto, a potential participant phoned me to ask about

the details. During the conversation I shared with her my personal situation, telling her that I had been remarried for about ten years. She asked, 'What does it feel like to be living in sin?' She actually believed that my second marriage was sinful because my former husband was still living. My own experience shows how theologically wrong this interpretation is. I think Jesus was attempting to show that all legislation about divorce is incomplete; he called us to ideal relationships that would make divorce unnecessary. In my second marriage the scars of divorce have been healed beyond description.

As I came out of illness after six years of separation, I was helped to see that the only way back to sound mental health was to recognize socially that my marriage could not be repaired. If I was to have any kind of a life, I had to recognize that the marriage was dead. I had to move toward a divorce. After going ahead with it, the possibility of my remarrying was extremely remote. Unlike the Old Testament practice of divorcing in order to remarry, I could not even think about letting myself in for another hurt. When I found a person who believed that there was a chance of building a new life without hurts, I had to rethink my traditional Anglican values concerning remarriage.

It was at this time that God's grace entered into my heart. I knew that the love I shared with my second husband was deeper than I could ever have imagined. The years have shown me the full meaning of Christ's ideal for man and woman. I experience daily what it means to be good for each other. There is no 'sin' left from my first marriage, except as it relates to my own personality. I am sure that Jesus did not intend people to remain in destructive relationships. Divorce is one way of recognising the spiritual death of a relationship. The importance of this part of the Christian gospel can never be underestimated. Christ did show the way to reconciliation in all matters and, most especially, in divorce.

*

In his book *Made in Heaven?* (SPCK, 1988) Canon Peter
Chambers writes about marrying again. Peter was Bishops'
Adviser for Marriage Education in the Church of England in the
1980s and is now a Canon of Sheffield Cathedral. While I was
working with Peter in London, he accompanied me on five years
of my journey to wholeness, was a rock and mainstay, and was
encouraging of my relationship with Bob.

> A person previously married may become attracted to a new
> partner, and may also wish to marry again. This may happen
> despite still unhappy memories of a previous marriage, or the
> untimely ending of a happy one: to be married again may
> offer relief from sadness and from the loneliness of being
> unmarried. People who have been married once have shown
> that they are disposed to marry; experience may caution them
> against a hasty decision to repeat marriage but time and
> attachment may overcome caution. There will be those for
> whom there can be no intention of a second marriage,
> whether it is because they are still attached to their former
> partner, or because to marry again would be against their per-
> sonal convictions, or because the first experience taught them
> that they are not willing and able to commit themselves to all
> that marriage entails. Those who decide to marry again will
> probably face some problems and demands that did not arise
> when they married for the first time. There may be continu-
> ing commitments that are consequences of a first marriage
> (for example maintenance, mortgage payments, care and con-
> trol of children, relationships with former parents-in-law and
> mutual friends). Such matters can be satisfactorily dealt with
> but often they are not properly resolved before a new mar-
> riage is entered upon. Other demands may be less obvious
> such as the emotional needs created by bereavement or
> divorce, or the need to deal with the continuing presence of
> the former spouse and his or her influence on events.
>
> The breakdown of a marriage is a series of events and even
> when it has culminated in divorce the partners are unlikely to
> have dealt with the emotional effect of the experience. When

people go through marriage breakdown, separation, divorce, living single and another marriage they may recognise peaks of emotional intensity, both along the way and later. These peaks may be associated with particular occasions: the decision to separate, actual separation, legal divorce, remarriage of either spouse, death of either spouse and the lifecycle transitions of children. For some people the process may feel like a roller coaster ride.

Even though a person may express a lot of grief at the time of a divorce, this will not usually complete the emotional process; but the more that is done at each peak-event, the less intense and disruptive will be the subsequent events. Among the feelings that may have to be dealt with are anger, sadness and confusion. The confusion may be created by transitory moods – feeling all right one day and deflated the next; ruminating about the past and thinking optimistically about the future; being resolved to manage life and lacking direction. Resolving this confusion may provide the confidence to marry again. Divorce occasions bereavement but without a body to bury. Divorce often proves to be a much more painful process than was ever imagined. Those who have undergone it may be cautious about risking it again and yet know that if divorce ever becomes necessary again they can survive it and will be better at doing so. This is the mentality with which a person *may* come to a second marriage. A person previously married may need to recognise what is left over from that marriage – feelings about the marriage and insights gained from it; feelings about their former partner; continuing relationships with, and responsibilities for, children. It is an event for which there are no clear guidelines and which is less clearly provided for by established rites of passage.

Reasons for marrying again

One very strong reason for wanting to marry again, already mentioned by Peter Chambers, is loneliness. This can take many forms, depending on one's lifestyle. At the beginning of my 'sin-

gle again' time I worked in a girls' boarding school. Long hours
and little free time, surrounded by 70 teenagers, meant that I
had no time to think about loneliness. But when I left the school
and went back to a secretarial post, although I was busy and
occupied every weekday with a full-time job, evenings and
weekends stretched interminably. I had no social life. Divorcees
whose children are still tiny or at school are lonely because of
the lack of adult company. There is no one to share opinions
with, talk about books or films, or whatever happens to be your
interest. It can also be hard to come to terms with having no
companionship with a member of the opposite sex. A mum with
young children can feel cut off from mainstream life, especially
if her own parents/family do not live nearby.

Going to restaurants or pubs is just not on for a woman alone
– especially in a big city, as I was. Social life can be practically
non-existent for a lone woman in a full-time occupation. Lack
of social contact is not good for humans. Even if we have a
totally absorbing job, we still need the stimulation of social
gatherings and contact with others outside our working envi-
ronment. We become emotionally vulnerable to offers of friendship, companionship, or more. Some will be genuine, but others
may not.

Reasons against marrying again

Our situation on our own, without sufficient close adult companionship, can lead to desperation. Desperation that never
again will we experience the closeness and warmth of a one-to-
one relationship with another person – especially a sexual relationship. Single people can feel like second-class citizens in the
face of everyone else's apparent 'coupleness'. The longing to be
part of the 'real world' again can be very powerful. But we
should beware. The longing can lead to disaster. Hasty remarriage, without proper consideration of all the ramifications,
even whether you actually *like* the person you are planning to
marry as opposed to liking the things you do together, can be a
journey to hell. If you have already been to hell on the road

from marriage breakdown to where you are now, you will not want to go there again. I cannot stress enough how cautious we must be about committing ourselves to a new marriage.

This is not intended to put anyone off marrying again. Far from it – that is why I have shown you that in my own case it has been a real joy and brought great happiness. What I have not said is that I could have made a dreadful mistake five years before I met Bob. At the same time as my divorce a friend's wife left him and they also were divorced. He and I spent several years walking the same path together. Although there was no romance, I had hopes that this might eventually lead 'somewhere'. Thankfully it did not. He left my new flat one day, having been very useful putting up curtain rails and doing other odd jobs, saying, 'Cheerio, see you around.' And that was it. I was devastated at the time, but realized later that we were totally unsuited. The relationship had run its course. It had been helpful to both of us; it needed to end.

I would like to tell you about a couple who married very soon after the husband's first wife died. Although this was not a divorce situation, there are many similarities between loss of a partner through death and marriage breakdown. The gap is huge for some and for this elderly man it was a dire situation. He just could not stand the loneliness, despite a loving son and grandchildren. Six months after his bereavement he met a lady, also widowed, of a similar age to himself, in a hotel bar. They got chatting and continued to meet for several weeks. He felt comforted by the female companionship and very quickly looked for something more. She was willing and not long afterwards they were married. The marriage took place in church though there was no overt sign that either of them was Christian (though they may well have been). At first the marriage was happy, although he had to make a lot of adjustments. His new wife was quite dissimilar to his first wife; she placed great emphasis on money and material goods. As time passed his happiness, along with his bank balance, decreased. His friends and relatives were uneasy. He fell ill and died when they had been married little more than ten years. Astoundingly, his will made no mention of his son and grandchildren, who were deprived of what is old-fashionedly called their 'birthright'; his widow was the beneficiary. He must have made the will himself, but his family are convinced that his wife influenced him, for her own gain. A cautionary tale, which should teach us to be very, very careful before making a commitment to a new marriage. There may be more at stake than our emotions.

What can be hoped for?

Much of this chapter is, understandably, based on my own experience, so this section will be about what I hoped for. You may have other expectations.

At those times when I thought about the possibility of marrying again, I was hoping to find someone who would provide companionship, love, kindness and humour. Notably I was not especially looking for other things, which came along with the package – the provision of a home (I became a property owner!) and a gentle and loving sexual relationship. Younger women may be hoping for different things – someone to share the upbringing of children, a provider, a champion in the trials of life and almost certainly a sexual partner. And I suppose, if one is young enough, the possibility of children.

The main hope for a new marriage must be that it will be happy. If we married young the first time, we will hope that experience will have taught us a great deal about life and relationships. We need to use what we have learned to ensure that we don't make the same mistakes again. What mistakes, you may ask. Well, I have never felt that I can push all the blame for the breakdown on to my former partner. We all make mistakes; sometimes it is because we are young and know no better. Other times we do know better, but still go ahead with faulty behaviour anyway. Chapter 6 may have revealed things you did not know about yourself. Use this knowledge to make sure that you know exactly who you are. That way, making a new marriage should not be a disaster, but a source of fulfilment. And make no mistake, I don't mean the new marriage will be roses all the way; Bob and I have our moments of irritation and annoyance; sometimes we have a good shout and then a good laugh afterwards. It is impossible to live closely with anyone without disagreement – just go with it and work through it. Minor conflict will not destroy your second marriage if you refuse to let it.

If you are contemplating marrying again don't be afraid to let God in on it. Just before Bob and I became engaged I did a five-day pilgrimage to Canterbury with a friend. On the last evening we went into that wonderful cathedral after the tourists had left and, armed with a candle each, made a pilgrimage of our own from place to place. We finished at the foot of Becket's steps and there, in the candlelight, I told God of my apprehension about my possible marriage, because Bob is Jewish. A response pinged straight into my mind – 'So was Jesus!' That clinched it. It was a moment I will never forget – in that moment God pointed me in the direction of happiness.

If one has good experiences of something it is natural to want to recommend it to others. As I say, we do occasionally have a mild disagreement, but we agree on the important things, the most important of which is that love should always be the arbiter of our behaviour – and not only in marriage. At the risk of becoming boring, it is worth repeating:

Love is patient and kind; love is not jealous or boastful; it is not arrogant or rude. Love does not insist on its own way; it is not irritable or resentful; it does not rejoice at wrong, but rejoices in the right. Love bears all things, believes all things, hopes all things, endures all things.

(1 Corinthians 13.4–7)

Living together outside marriage

This chapter would not be complete without mentioning that many couples decide to set up home together without getting married. This is something I seriously considered before marrying Bob but discarded because it felt 'right' to get married. There was, however, a small financial disadvantage to marrying again which has affected my state pension. I was aware of this and decided the benefits outweighed the losses and went ahead with the marriage with, as I have said, no regrets.

There are many couples, either divorced or widowed, who happily live together for the rest of their lives without marriage. This will be a problem for some people and churches where biblical laws are rigidly adhered to. In one case a lady in such a relationship who wished to join one of her local churches was advised by the minister not to apply. He explained that the whole congregation took part in voting for new church members and they were likely to refuse her application because she was living with her partner outside marriage. He thought it better for her to avoid this public embarrassment.

For some couples there can be considerable financial loss involved in marrying again. Others, having had a bad experience of marriage, find it too hard to commit to another marriage. One couple told me that not being married did not mean there was no commitment to their relationship, but in the (unlikely) event of it failing, they could not face the long legal wrangling and bitterness they had experienced during their divorces. Their present arrangement is a form of self-protection. Their trust has been badly damaged and they do not wish to risk more hurt. The female partner had experienced weeks of legal argument in the courts, being made to feel like a 'criminal', and suffering insults from 'nasty' solicitors. It is hardly surprising that she and her new partner were reluctant to undertake marriage again.

We have to trust that the Lord knows our innermost feelings; He will know the depth of our commitment to a new partner, married or unmarried. If an arrangement feels right and good for the couple involved, others should not make judgements. Only God can do that and if He wishes to give His blessing and grace, that is between Him and the couple. Our human judgements will often fall short of God's. My own belief is that love must be the overriding factor. If we treat one another in the most loving way we can, this will lead to actions that are true to what our heavenly Father wants for us.

*

Make time for stillness and quiet –
To listen to the Spirit –
Who makes everything new.

Conclusion

Because this book probably raises more questions than it answers, I am not going to attempt to come to any conclusions – it is up to each of us to do that for ourselves. We are all individual and what might be right for one person will not necessarily be right for another. Instead, I want to share two concerns. The first is the lack of a liturgy or ritual within the churches for Christians faced with the legal ending of their marriage, providing a means whereby they can feel released and remain true to their faith. The second arises from something Laura wrote. She suggests there may be such a thing as 'Christian divorce'.

A service for the ending of a marriage

By making decisions about marrying divorced people in church before offering them a form of service which could provide a release from their former vows and an opportunity for repentance and forgiveness before moving on, the Church is putting the cart before the horse. For many people the prospect of marrying again is something which they cannot countenance; they still consider themselves married to their ex-partner in the eyes of both God and the Church. The marriage which they made has ended, and although many churches are now willing to marry them to a new partner, there has been no official acknowledgement by the Church of the ending of their marriage. A liturgy designed as a closure of the failed relationship would also express the Church's assurance of its continuing care for divorced people and of God's love for them.

There are clergy who will conduct such a service, for a lone partner or for the couple, either on their own or in the presence of family and friends, but because of the lack of provision of a suitable liturgy these services are inevitably 'home-made' – by the priest or the divorced persons themselves. Until such time as the Church fully accepts marriage breakdown openly and honestly, this situation will not change.

One woman, on finding that her need for a closure on her marriage was not available in the Anglican Church, devised her own service. These are her suggestions of what it could contain:

- an opportunity for lamentation;
- prayers to God for mercy and for help, a statement about God's compassion;
- an invitation to the separated/divorced person to say to God what they needed to say; this might or might not be termed 'confession' in a strict sense, it would depend on the circumstances;
- the response of the divorced person;
- a prayer by the officiant, perhaps absolution, or a prayer for strength and healing, an affirmation and invitation to a new life;
- an opportunity for thanksgiving by the divorced person;
- a short period of silence;
- prayers for the children of the marriage, if any, and for friends, family and the divorced person, followed by prayers for protection and other prayers as desired;
- a blessing;
- Eucharist to follow, if desired (or the laying on of hands, or both).

(Anne Tanner in *Treasures of Darkness*)

Until such time as the churches provide a form of service people will continue to write their own. These will all be different because we are different. There are various options for telling God, through the Church, about the ending of one's marriage. Some parts of the burial service lend themselves to such modification. Healing services may contain useful material. When writing such a service for ourselves we need to ensure that the ritual is powerful enough to carry the depth of feeling being discharged through it.

The lack of such provision by the churches may be due to a fear that such a ritual will encourage easy divorce. I do not believe so, but rather that, along with the churches' support for separated and divorced people, it would reinforce the love of God, shown by the Church in action as it upholds and affirms those who might otherwise be wandering in a wilderness, uncertain of their place in God's family.

Can divorce ever be Christian?

You may share my confused thoughts about 'Christian marriage'. Writing the chapter with that heading has not led me to any firm conclusions, and I don't suppose it has cleared things up for most readers either. Laura, the lady with the guilty secret, sent me an article she had written about her marriage and divorce entitled 'Through Christian Marriage to Christian Divorce'. The following is the gist of what Laura wrote.

Laura and her husband were 19 and 21 when they fell in love. The courtship was not always smooth – there were a number of partings and reconciliations before they married three years later. Laura was brought up in a Christian home but her faith was very childlike. Her husband became a Christian as a young adult. They became lovers early on in the courtship.

In spite of the marriage being somewhat volatile, the early years were happy. However, there were puzzling and worrying aspects caused by what, with maturity, Laura sees as being due to marrying without first discovering their partner's expectations of the relationship. His seemed to Laura to be higher and more demanding than hers and she felt that in many ways he never found the marriage really satisfactory or entirely acceptable.

Laura goes on to describe her realization that over the years her unconfessed adultery had changed their relationship – because the guilt had changed her. Her husband 'threw himself into his work' and their relationship deteriorated. Eventually, after a year when communication was non-existent, except on the most superficial level, in an effort to repair the marriage she felt it was time to confess her adultery to her husband. Failing to understand her motives he pressed her in the erroneous belief that she had more to confess. There followed weeks of agony going over old hurts and fears, searching for the truth about their relationship. This apparently worked and they had what Laura describes as 'six months of an idyllic marriage'. Then, without warning, it all crumbled again and her husband fell in love with someone else.

Laura's attempts to salvage the marriage were hopeless. Her love for him and her children, her belief that she was to blame for the problems, and her Christian faith, all led her to leave their home, hoping a separation would bring them together again. Sadly this did not happen. Six months after she left, he divorced her. She did not contest the action and, although shattered and heartbroken, remained convinced that God was with her and there was a purpose in life for her.

Laura added a rider to this, written six years after the divorce, in which she says she no longer felt the need to take the biggest share of the 'blame' for the breakdown. She concluded, 'My life has proved happier and more fulfilling than I imagined possible and for that I thank God.'

The concept of Christian divorce creates a conflict between psychology and spirituality, reality and ideals. I am not sure whether I can go along altogether with Laura's notion of a Christian divorce, but she may well be right and many will readily agree with her. It is certainly possible for two Christian people to conduct their divorce in the most loving and non-confrontational way possible, and in that sense I suppose it is Christian divorce. There is biblical precedent for divorce, as Glad Bryce has said, for the purpose of making another marriage. If Laura's husband wished to have a divorce in order to marry someone else, then it could be said that he was behaving in accordance with biblical precedent. The whole question of divorce for Christians is a theological muddle and one that may never be satisfactorily resolved, although the 'stumbling block' theory mentioned in Chapter 4, about who actually joins a couple in marriage, may provide part of the answer. In the meantime we must do the best we can and hope and pray that God will be with us in our attempts to reconcile our 'falling short' with the ideal our Christian faith holds before us.

*

Immediately following divorce the future can look bleak, shrouded in mist, or even completely non-existent. The basic practicalities of life take priority. There is little time to think or worry about other areas of being 'single again'; going to church, or saying one's prayers, can be put on hold until we 'have more time'. But we cannot get rid of God as easily as that. We might think we have lost Him, left Him somewhere in a happier past, but He is still around. It is a matter of searching, often in surprising places. He has an uncanny knack of turning up when we least expect Him. When we would rather He stayed away until we are ready, or have more time, or can find peace and quiet.

However bleak things may look, God is no deserter. He will use the new situation and our brokenness to heal and to point us to a new path, leading to new purposes, new fulfilment.

I hope that now you have reached this point you agree with me that there is life after divorce. Being 'single again' can be a positive or negative experience. Negative experiences lead to negative lifestyles. It is in our own interests to find positive ways of relating to the world and people around us, otherwise we will waste all the experience we have had. How we do that will depend greatly on our personal image of God. That image will affect our decisions, our emotions, our perception of what God wants for us. I can only make decisions for myself. I am the one who knows how I see God and how I relate to Him. If nothing else, I hope that you will now have a firmer image of God in your mind so that as you move forward into the future you can speak to Him and share with Him your deepest feelings. In return He will guide you through whatever you face, however difficult. He is waiting for you to ask Him.

Further reading

Bell, Hannah, *Pierced to the Heart*, Pickering Paperbacks, 1984

Common Worship: Services and Prayers for the Church of England, Church House Publishing, 2000

Furlong, Monica, *One Woman's View*, The Mothers' Union, 1981

Green, Wendy, *The Christian and Divorce*, Mowbray, 1981

The Rite Lines, quarterly newsletter of Broken Rites, 1983–2003

Standing Committee of the General Synod, *Marriage and the Standing Committee's Task*, CIO Publishing, 1983

Tanner, Anne, *Treasures of Darkness: Struggling with Separation and Divorce in the Church*, Anglican Book Centre, Toronto, 1990

Thatcher, Adrian, *The Daily Telegraph Guide to Christian Marriage and to Getting Married in Church*, Continuum, 2003

Working Party of the Board for Social Responsibility, *Something to Celebrate: Valuing Families in Church and Society*, Church House Publishing, 1995

Working Party of the Synod's Standing Committee, *An Honourable Estate: The Doctrine of Marriage According to English Law. The Obligation of the Church to Perform Marriages*, Church House Publishing, 1988

Helpful addresses

(Also see your local telephone directory or local library)

Broken Rites
Secretary
93 York Road
Teddington
Middlesex TW11 8SL
Tel: 020 8943 4688
Email: secretary@brokenrites.org
Website: www.brokenrites.org
(Non-denominational support group for separated and
divorced wives of clergy)

Al-Anon Family Groups
61 Great Dover Street
London SE1 4YF
Tel: 020 7403 0888
Email: alanonuk@aol.com
Website: www.al-anonuk.org.uk

Alcoholics Anonymous
Box 1
Stonebow House
Stonebow
York YO1 1NJ
National helpline: 0845 769 7555

Anglican Marriage Encounter
David and Liz Percival
11 Lambourne Close
Sandhurst
Berks GU47 8JL
Tel: 01344 779658
Website: www.2-in-2-1.co.uk

Baptist Expression of Marriage Encounter
Bill and Brenda Reynolds
26 Bellingdon Road
Chesham
Bucks HP5 2HA
Tel: 01494 782466
Website: www.beofme.org.uk

Care for the Family
PO Box 488
Cardiff CF15 7YY
Tel: 029 2081 0800
Email: mail@ccf.org.uk
Website: www.care-for-the-family.org.uk
(Christian organization that promotes strong family life and care for those hurting because of family breakdown)

Churches Ministerial Counselling Service
Administrator: Revd Ian Millgate
C/o Baptist House
PO Box 44
129 Broadway
Didcot OX11 8RT
Tel: 01235 517705
Email: admin@cmcs.org.uk
Website: www.cmcs.org.uk
(A 'Free Churches' service for ministers, Salvation Army offi-cers and some others in pastoral ministry and all adult mem-bers of their immediate household)

DivorceCare
Merrily Richie
57a Windsor Road
Forest Gate
London E7 0QY
Tel: 020 8534 7339
(Help as you recover from the pain of separation and divorce)

FLAME (Family Life and Marriage Education)
Robert Runcie House
60 Marsham Street
Maidstone
Kent ME14 1EW
Tel: 01622 755014
Email: flame@csr.org.uk
(Anglican organization for support in family life and marriage)

Lesbian and Gay Christian Movement
Oxford House
Derbyshire Street
London E2 6HG
Tel: 020 7739 1249
Email: lgcm@lgcm.org.uk
Website: www.lgcm.org.uk

Marriage Care
1 Blythe Mews
Blythe Road
London W14 0NW
Tel: 020 7371 1341
National helpline: 0845 660 6000
Email: Marriagecare@btinternet.com
Website: www.marriagecare.org.uk
(Formerly for Catholic clients but now non-denominational)

Relate
Herbert Gray College
Little Church Street
Rugby
Warwickshire CV21 3AP
Tel: 01788 573241
Email: enquiries@relate.org.uk
Website: www.relate.org.uk
(Also see local telephone directory and/or library)

The Samaritans
National helpline: 08457 90 90 90
Email: Jo@samaritans.org
Website: www.samaritans.org.uk
(Also see local telephone directory)

Worldwide Marriage Encounter
(Roman Catholic)
John and Brenda Levesley
40 June Crescent
Bolehall
Tamworth
Staffs B77 3BH
Tel: 01827 65651
Website: www.wwme.org.uk

Acknowledgements

The author wishes to express her thanks to the following for granting permission to reproduce material of which they are the publisher or copyright holder:

Excerpts from *Divorce and Spiritual Growth* © 1982 by Anglican Book Centre, 600 Jarvis Street, Toronto, ON, Canada M4Y 2J6. Used with permission.

SPCK, London, extracts from *Made in Heaven?* (New Library of Pastoral Care) by Peter Chambers, 1988.

Extract from 'Meekness and Majesty' – Administered by worshiptogether.com songs excluding UK and Europe, administered by Kingsway Music. Used by permission.

The Editor of *Crucible* (October–December 2003), extracts from articles 'More Light on "Issues in Human Sexuality"' by Kenneth Jennings and 'Homosexuality as a factor in clergy marriage breakdown' by Christine McMullen. G. J. Palmer & Sons.

Sarah Thorley for permission to use her poems 'Decree Absolute', 'Lonely', 'And Yet' and 'Memories'.